The Master Book for
Lean Six Sigma Green Belt Certification

CSSGB Comprehensive Study Guide for Certification Exams and Job Interviews

Nilakantasrinivasan J
Canopus Business Management Group

For details contact:
Canopus Business Management Group www.collaborat.com
No.1, Anna Street, Ponniamman Nagar +91 9176615766
Ayanambakkam, littlebook@collaborat.com
Chennai - 600095
India

Foreword

Are you looking for a compendium of references on Lean Six Sigma that is a comprehensive guide with answers for the questions that arise – this book is for you. *The Master Book for Lean Six Sigma Green Belt Certification* is a good companion to help assimilate your learning. Structured in a simple Question and Answer format, it is easy on the reader in getting answers from a practical stand point, for day to day application of concepts, certification or preparing for job interviews.

Lean Six Sigma Certification boosts career progression, from my own personal experience. However, preparation for Certification can be quiet daunting. While too many aids are available, this book covers all the topics of ASQ and IASSC Green Belt Body of Knowledge.
As a certified in Lean Six Sigma Green Belt holder – you are expected to know the concepts and also be able to answer in job interviews. This Q&A format, with relevant examples and infographics, comes handy in preparing for such job interviews.

I have known Neil both professionally as well as on a personal front for more than fifteen years. He has contributed significantly to the process management community through various training programs that lead to certification, custom projects or advisory initiatives. I am sure you will enjoy referring to this book in your Lean Six Sigma journey.

Hussain Thameezdeen
Head of Operations
Qatar First Bank

Purpose of the Book

In my experience of coaching over 3000 candidates for Lean Six Sigma Certifications and having interviewed over 300 candidates for Lean Six Sigma roles, one thing I can say with conviction is that *Six Sigma is overwhelming and a difficult subject when it comes to answers questions in exams or in interviews.* While many practitioners understand the concepts of Lean Six Sigma, they fail to give 'right' answers in these instances. They fail to create the right impression in the interview. Instead, they leave an impression of mere familiarity, which doesn't make the cut either in Interviews or Exams.

Why this book?

While preparing for CSSGB exams of ASQ & IASSC, a learner like you encounters a lot of doubt. If you have to clear exams, you should have crystal clear understanding of all the concepts and you should know to paraphrase it in the right way. Whether you are taking objective or subjective type exams, these are critical aspects.

- As a result, this book is structured in the form of Q & A.
- All necessary concepts are explained with examples across industries. In interviews, interviewers test application knowledge; I have seen candidates drawing a blank when you ask them for an example.
- It is comprehensive and covers all the necessary topics that a CSSGB needs to know. It is drawn based on universal curriculum that maps to both ASQ & IASSC Body of Knowledge.

How to use this book?

- While preparing for CSSGB exams, reading the book sequentially will help
- Before an interview, you can brush up the topics of your choice

Structure of this Book?

As this is an in-depth study material, it is voluminous. Thus the content is split into 3 parts. While Part 1 covers, Six Sigma Overview & Define Phase, Part 2 covers Measure, Part 3 Analyze, Improve & Control phases.

Further reading?

If you wish to learn about various application aspects, tips and practical nitty-gritties, you will find out online learning courses invaluable.

For more details visit: www.SixSigmaCertificationCourse.com or www.Collaborat.com

All the best!

Nilakantasrinivasan (Neil)

Part One
Six Sigma Overview & Define Phase

Contents

1 Fundamentals of Six Sigma

Understanding Six Sigma

The Six Sigma is an approach to business process improvement and performance management which encompasses a statistical and method-driven process. In order to effectively deploy the process in your organization, it is necessary to identify the basic elements that drive the Six Sigma methodology. Knowledge of the Six Sigma fundamentals is the first step toward a successful Six Sigma implementation. Before applying any business strategy in an organization, you must identify the goals and benefits of the strategy. You must also recognize the need for such a business strategy in the organization.

What is the definition of Six Sigma?

Six Sigma is a process improvement approach that strives to enhance the quality and efficiency of process outputs by eliminating the causes of defects and variation in a process. Sigma (σ) is a Greek letter that represents standard deviation and is used by statisticians to measure process variation.

Six Sigma is a customer-focused approach that aims at achieving increased bottom line profitability. Its goal is for a near perfection or zero defects. The driving forces behind Six Sigma are the complete grasp of customer requirements, data-driven, decision-making and statistical analysis that promotes the improvement of business processes in an organization.

Let's understand this with an example. Assume John Smith, a manager at Janrex Inc., realizes that there has been a substantial increase in customer complaints about the products developed by his company. He calls for further investigation, which reveals loopholes in the overall product development process, leading to inconsistencies in the final product. The product development process needs to be addressed using an appropriate improvement approach. For this purpose, John chooses the Six Sigma approach, which focuses on improving the process by reducing defects in the product.

What are the important terms associated with Six Sigma?

Here are some of the common terms used in Six Sigma:

- **Standard Deviation** - *Standard deviation* is a statistical measure of variation from the mean in a distribution or set of data.
- **DPMO** - Defects Per Million Opportunities (DPMO) is the average number of defects across a million opportunities.
- **Defects** - Any product, service, or parameter that fails to meet customer requirements is considered a defect. Therefore, defects are undesirable and efforts should be made to reduce them and improve customer satisfaction. In fact, a Six Sigma quality performance indicates less than 3.4 defects per million opportunities.

- **Process Variation -** If a process or a set of processes delivers variable outputs, then the variation is called process variation. For example, a manufacturer will source raw materials from various suppliers. However, in instances, where different suppliers supply the same raw material, the quality may vary from one supplier to another. This variation in quality of the input may cause variation in output quality. This variation is called process variation.

- **Process Sigma Level -** Before improving a process, it is necessary to understand the Sigma level of the process you are trying to improve. The Sigma level will give a short-term internal estimate that will predict the long-term Sigma level for the process and provide an estimate of the effort needed to achieve the Six Sigma level. Additionally, Sigma levels—such as Sigma 1, Sigma 2, Sigma 3, Sigma 4, Sigma 5, and Sigma 6—will provide a consistent method of comparing different processes and critical activities. They provide a measure to see how well or how poorly a process performs.

What is the need for Six Sigma?

Surviving in a business world that is full of competition is crucial to any organization. Six Sigma provides the means to handle declining product prices in the market, which helps any organization, compete with the best companies in business. It targets zero defects by setting a common performance goal for the entire organization. Six Sigma helps an organization achieve increased profitability and quality improvement rates, ahead of any of its competitors. Reduced scrap-related costs, rework, improved yield, and increased customer satisfaction are identified in companies striving to achieve Six Sigma.

A Six Sigma initiative differs from other quality improvement methodologies because it ensures that the costs involved in implementation are offset by the gains received from improvements.

What do we mean by Six Sigma Philosophy?

The Six Sigma philosophy considers any "work" as a process that requires inputs to produce outputs and asserts that variations in the quality of the output (Y) can be reduced by controlling the inputs (X). It looks at a process as one that can be defined, measured, analysed, improved, and then controlled and is expressed as $Y = f(X)$.

What are the Goals of Six Sigma?

The primary goal of Six Sigma is to implement a measurement-based strategy in an organization that concentrates on process improvement and reducing variation. In addition to this, the other important goals of Six Sigma include:
- Reducing the number of defects, leading to the improved quality of a product or service.
- Achieving customer satisfaction by ensuring that customer expectations are met.
- Reducing cycle time, which enables the faster delivery of products.
- And, higher profitability by improving efficiency and effectiveness of the organization.

Explain about the evolution of Six Sigma?

Six Sigma is a combination of the best elements of various quality improvement methodologies and a rigorous statistic-driven approach to performance improvement. The term "Six Sigma" was coined by Bill Smith, an engineer at Motorola. Six Sigma, in the present form, originated in the early 1980s at Motorola as a tool for reducing product-failure levels by 10 times in five years. General Electric (GE) implemented Six Sigma in 1995 after Motorola, and Allied Signal followed the Six Sigma trail after GE.

Six Sigma methodology evolved by combining the best elements of earlier quality improvement innovations.

Innovation	Description
Uniformity system	<ul><li>Introduced by Eli Whitney in 1798</li><li>Created a necessity for measuring dimensions</li><li>Evolved into specifications</li></ul>
Moving assembly line	<ul><li>Introduced by Henry Ford in 1913</li><li>Highlighted the importance of part consistency</li><li>Led to the sampling method, replacing 100% inspection</li></ul>
Control charts	<ul><li>Introduced by Walter Shewhart in 1924</li><li>Signaled the age of statistical quality control</li></ul>
Quality movement	<ul><li>Introduced by the Japanese in 1945</li><li>Pioneered the usage of data to quantify variation</li><li>Ensures integration of quality across all levels of an organization</li></ul>
Customer Centric Products	<ul><li>Japanese focused on eliminating defects and reducing cycle time</li><li>Resulted in production of high-quality, efficient, and customer-centric products</li></ul>
.Zero defects	<ul><li>Was introduced by Philip Crosby in 1980</li><li>Led to perfection in a product, process, or service is attainable.</li></ul>
Quality standards	<ul><li>Introduced by the International Organization for Standardization (ISO) in 1987</li><li>Led to uniformity in quality practices across countries</li></ul>
Six Sigma	<ul><li>Motorola wins the first Malcolm Baldrige National Quality Award in 1987</li><li>Led to the present Six Sigma methodology</li></ul>

What is the definition of Process?

A *process* is a set of structured activities or tasks that produce a specific output or a product that meets customer requirements or specifications. The customer is the beneficiary of a process, and therefore, it is a sequence of activities that convert one or more inputs into a specific output that is of value to the customer. A process may lead to a sequence of interrelated processes where the culmination of one process is the start of another.

What are Process Inputs?

Process inputs can be data, services, or material that a process converts into outputs. The recipient of a process input is the process itself. Generally, a process can have several inputs, and if you consider an organization as a single process, then the components, dimensions and process settings can be considered process inputs.

If the process is developed according to the goals of Six Sigma, process inputs, referred to by the term "X," are the focus of attention because they are vital for the output to meet customer specifications.

Process inputs are also referred to as Key Performance Input Variables (KPIVs), or the independent variables, causes, problems, or metrics, which can be controlled.

What are Process Outputs?

A *process output* is the material, service, or data that results from the operation of a process. The recipient of a process is normally the customer or the client. In some processes, outputs are used as inputs for the next stage of the process or for a different process. Generally, a process can result in more than one output, and if an organization is considered a single process, then the final product is their primary output. If the process is developed as per the goals of Six Sigma, then the process output, referred to by the term "Y," is a good measure of customer requirements. If the process consistently delivers on the output metric, then customer requirements are met.

Process outputs are also referred to as Key Performance Output Variables (KPOV), or the dependent variables, effects, symptoms, or metrics, which will be monitored.

·····

Identify Organizational Drivers and Metrics

To identify the right process for your performance improvement efforts, it is important to identify the key business drivers and performance metrics of your organization.

In this topic, you will identify the key business drivers and metrics that impact an organization. Key drivers and metrics are the basis by which organizations evolve their business and performance goals. Identifying them will enable you to focus your performance improvement efforts on business processes that will have maximum impact.

What are Organizational Processes?

Organizational processes are a set of core processes that make an organization effective, efficient, and adaptable. These core processes are focused on delivering the right quality of products or services to customers, per their requirements. Core processes may differ from one organization to another and are dependent on the organizational structure.

Example: A manufacture of semiconductor devices.

A manufacturer of semiconductor devices, such as transducers and load cells, sources raw materials from their vendors. The material and resource requirement planning include inward and outward logistics. Inward logistics include in-warding material in stores, moving from supply to the production line in a timely manner, and storing raw materials. Outward logistics include dispatching finished goods and forming a part of an organizational process called supply chain management. This process cuts across different departments, geographies, and products that the organization manufactures.

What are Sub-Processes?

Core processes are supported by sub-processes, which enable them to achieve higher customer satisfaction, better product quality, and increased delivery and time to market speed. In a manufacturing environment, these sub-processes are performed in a sequence that enables effective and efficient completion of a manufacturing process.

What are some examples of Sub-Process?

- **Purchase -** To increase profitability of a business by procuring high-quality raw materials at the most cost-effective price and by optimizing the inventory cost of raw materials.
- **Production -** To process raw materials efficiently and produce high yields by reducing defects and rework. Attention is paid to training and reducing machine downtime through suitable maintenance programs for the production machinery.
- **Sales and marketing -** Innovative strategies are employed as part of public relations. Advertising and sales campaigns are used to increase the willingness of a customer to buy manufactured products.
- **Delivery -** Care is taken to process the order quickly, freeze the scheduled time of delivery, and ensure that the delivery schedule is met in the most cost-effective manner. Obtaining customer feedback is a key element in this sub-process.

What are Organizational Drivers?

Organizational drivers are the highest level of measure in a business process. They are strongly linked to the strategic goals of an organization. Organizations depend heavily on them for measuring performance. If the key drivers of an organization are achieved, then the organization can be considered to have achieved its overall goal set for that period. Usually, organizational goals are defined for a three-to five-year time frame.

Organizational drivers are usually business-level metrics, such as financial and performance measures. Other organizational drivers are customer, market, product, and supplier related. They form the backbone of any business effort to improve customer, operational, and financial performance. Some organizations go with just one strategic goal. Others have more, but limit the number of goals to five at the maximum. Because a measurement system is established to measure the progress of the strategic goals, these strategic goals are referred to as the Big Y and are considered outputs in operational processes. These organizational drivers are in turn linked to the downstream key metrics of processes.

What are Metrics?

Metrics are process-level and operational-level measures of efficiency and effectiveness of processes. Only efficient processes can help an organization meet the three- to five-year strategic goal. Gauging the organization and its processes is dependent on the selection and use of these metrics. These operational and process-level metrics are considered the Xs and inputs for the organizational drivers, which are regarded as the Big Y.

Compared to organizational drivers, metrics are more tactical in nature, are measured more often, and can be easily impacted. Because X is considered the input for achieving the Big Y, an organization will achieve the Big Y by monitoring and controlling X.

Operational-level metrics are measures that relate to the efficiency or effectiveness of cost, performance, time, and much more. They provide inputs to constantly gauge the effectiveness and efficiency of process improvement efforts.

What is Balanced Scorecard?

A *Balanced Scorecard (BSC)* is a strategic performance management framework for measuring the impact of strategic decisions across all organizational drivers of an organization. A BSC provides a wider perspective on strategic decisions made by an organization by measuring the impact on key business drivers such as finance, customer requirements, internal processes, innovation, and growth perspectives.

The BSC was conceived with the intent to overcome the limitations of traditional performance measurement tools. At the basic level, managers utilize it to track the activities of their direct reports and monitor the impact of their actions. At the decision-making level, a BSC is used both as a tool that facilitates strategic decision-making and as one that provides an insight into future performances.

Share an example of Balanced Scorecard?

An automobile manufacturer embraced BSC as a way to remain competitive in a rapidly evolving sector. The ensuing benchmarks show how BSC permeated into each department to coordinate the delivery of quality products and the ability to offer diverse models.

Financial Perspective-How does the organization look to resource providers?	Customer Perspective-How do customers view the organization?
• Profitability-percent excess revenue and percent of net revenue • Efficiency-efficient processing of raw materials • Leverage-total debt to total assets	• Understand needs • Ease of ordering • Variety/availability • Professional • Courteous
Internal Process Perspective – Is the organization productive and effective?	**Innovation and Learning Perspective-How do employees view the organization?**
• Operation and maintenance perspective • Suitability of equipment and procedures to achieve defined targets and objectives • Appropriateness of the training given to key personal	• Influence in the community • Know how to use tools • Manage Workload • Advancement opportunities • Valuable training

What are the different Six Sigma Improvement Methodologies?

There are two basic Six Sigma models: DMAIC (Define, Measure, Analyze, Improve, and Control) and DFSS (Design for Six Sigma), also known as DMADV (Define, Measure, Analyze, Design, and Verify). These methodologies use a measurement-based strategy to achieve the Six Sigma objectives of process improvement and variation reduction.

- **DMAIC** is used to add incremental improvements to an existing process.
- **DFSS** is used to develop new processes, services, or products when existing process require more than just incremental improvements.
- **JDI** is another method for problem solving. In a continuous improvement process where rigorous methodologies, such as DMAIC, are not required, **JDI** (Just Do It) method of problem solving is deployed. Though JDI is considered a shortcut approach to process improvement, it is used in instances where management believes it has sufficient information to bypass or shorten the Measure or Analyze phase. JDI is also deployed in instances when the process improvement team wants to demonstrate immediate results. It is used to reduce data collection and analysis effort and move on to the execution stage; thus saving time and effort.

How can your organization benefit by implementing Six Sigma?

Answers will vary, but may include increased profit margins by reducing costs and growing revenue, improved business performance due to the reduction of variations and defects, reduced delivery time due to reduced manufacturing lead time, enhanced customer satisfaction due to better quality, expanded capacity in terms of productivity without spending on additional resources, accelerated improvement processes by leveraging the "prescriptive" approach of Lean, leveraged data analysis and statistical tools of Six Sigma for making process improvements and sustaining these improvements, and leveraged Six Sigma methodologies for better results.

What do you think are the most significant goals of Six Sigma?

Answers will vary, but may include aligning the organization to customer needs, improving profitability, and reducing variations and defects and by identifying Six Sigma Methodologies.

What do you understand by TQM?

Total Quality Management (TQM) is a structured system focused on satisfying customers by involving all members of an organization in improving the quality of products, processes, and resources. Sustained customer satisfaction, its main objective, is accomplished through systematic methods for problem solving, breakthrough achievement, and standardization derived from teaching quality leaders such as Philip B. Crosby, W. Edwards Deming, Armand V. Feigenbaum, Kaoru Ishikawa, and Joseph M. Juran. There are no hard-line procedures for implementing TQM. The PDCA cycle, also known as the Shewhart Cycle or the Deming Cycle, is a popular TQM problem-solving tool.

Describe PDCA cycle of TQM?

PDCA (The Plan-Do-Check-Act) cycle involves four basic steps for carrying out continuous improvement in a process. Four basic steps of PDCA:

- **Plan** - Recognize the opportunity for process improvement and identify the plan for improvement.
- **Do** - The plan is implemented. Simultaneously, employees are trained, and activities such as scheduling and follow-up happen. If the desired process improvement is not achieved, the plan is abandoned and the improvement effort will start from the planning stage.
- **Check** - The implementation of the action plan will yield results. These results are then compared with the planned results. Deviations are recorded and an improvement plan is proposed to achieve results.
- **Act** - On the results of the check step, and a decision is made whether to restart PDCA or standardize on the results.

. . . . .

Describe Project Selection and Organizational Goals

In the previous topic, you identified organizational drivers and metrics and determined their impact on the entire organization. You also need to be able to evaluate Six Sigma projects and align them to your organizational goals.

Identifying suitable Six Sigma projects and determining when to deploy them are important for an organization's sustainability and eventual success. Consequently, implementing Six Sigma on an ineffective project will impact the success of the project but bring little change to the organization's bottom line. Therefore, it is important for you to identify the right project and understand the degree of its impact on the organization.

Project selection process will be covered in Lesson 3 in detail along with Define tools.

■ ■ ■ ■ ■

Describe Lean

In the earlier topic, you described the project selection process and the key Six Sigma methodologies. The Lean manufacturing methodology has made significant contributions to the Six Sigma approach. In this topic, you will identify the elements of Lean. While implementing Six Sigma, the key concepts, applications, and principles of Lean are important because various line positions have specific responsibilities. Along with an understanding of the Six Sigma principles, an awareness of Lean manufacturing principles will provide you with a holistic view of the Six Sigma implementation.

What are the goals of Lean?

Lean manufacturing has a few important goals, which have led many industries to implement. Lean in their production processes. The goals include:

- Improving quality to stay ahead of competition in the market. This is done by capturing customer requirements and redesigning operational processes to meet those requirements.
- Eliminating waste to make processes more efficient. This is done by eliminating activities that do not add any value to the product or service.
- Reducing variability and inconsistencies by standardizing processes and outputs.
- And, reducing costs by ensuring that production does not exceed customer demands. By preventing overproduction, organizations can also make sure that inventory costs do not increase.

Describe the key principles of Lean?

The implementation of Lean techniques in an organization is guided by a few important principles.

Principle	Description
Value	Defining the value
Value stream	Identifying the value stream
Flow	Creating flow in the value stream
Pull	Creating pull in the value stream
Perfection	Creating a continuous improvement culture
Leveling	Creating a balanced workflow
Standardized processes	Developing standards and following them
Kanban	Using a visual signaling system
Visual control	Using visual control methods
Quick changeover	Enabling the reduction of time
Defect prevention	Reducing the cost of poor quality

What is Kaizen?

Kaizen is an approach that focuses on continuous, simple, and small improvements to business processes rather than a few major and complex improvements or re-engineering initiatives. It is a combination of two words in Japanese—"kai," which means "change," and "zen," which means "good." In simple terms, it means "change for the better" and in a business context, it signifies "improvement."

Kaizen is applied in different processes across different industries. It involves all employees in an organization—managers and workers alike. Teamwork, personal discipline, improved morale, quality circles, and suggestions for improvement are regarded as the five major elements of Kaizen.

Share an example of Kaizen in detail?

A tool and die department has been receiving several complaints about delays in the delivery of tools and even missing dies. Upon investigation, it was found that they were often misplaced and considerable time was spent searching for them, leading to delays and missing items. To set things right, management decided to adopt Kaizen.

As part of the Kaizen initiative, the following steps were taken:
- Old and outdated tools and dies were removed and placed in storage.
- New pieces were sorted and arranged in different racks based on the part numbers.

- Every store keeper was given a kit of necessary tools so that he or she did not have to waste time searching for the items.
- And, the entire office layout was redesigned to provide a better workspace for tool and die makers.

What is 5S?

The 5S methodology includes five steps that help organizations create and maintain an organized, clean, and safe work environment as part of their initiative to implement Lean.

- Sort - Involves determining necessary and unnecessary tasks, raw materials, finished goods, and tools in a process. As a result of this step, all unnecessary tasks in the process are discarded.
- Set in place - Involves arranging and labelling necessary tasks, raw materials, finished goods, and tools in a process so that they are easy to locate and use.
- Shine - Focuses on keeping machines and work environments clean.
- Standardize - Focuses on extending cleanliness and continuously practicing the first three steps of the 5S methodology.
- Sustain - Encourages implementing the 5S methodology on an ongoing basis by establishing required standards and strategies.

Describe Error Proofing.

Error proofing is a tool, also referred to as *mistake proofing* or *poka-yoke,* used to prevent the occurrence of defects and ensure that mistakes are accurately detected when problems occur. Error proofing allows a process to proceed further only when all issues are resolved. Thus, error proofing helps to improve process throughout and quality and reduce defect and rework rates.

Example: Error Proofing in Turn Signals of Cars.

Turn signals of cars are automatically cut off when the driver completes the turn. This method of error proofing in cars helps prevent major accidents because drivers tend to forget to turn off the turn signal. When a turn signal is left on, it can send the wrong message to other drivers on the road and lead to accidents.

What do you understand by Value Stream Mapping?

Value stream mapping is the process of evaluating different activities that exist in the production process and identifying value-adding and non-value -adding activities. This is done by creating a current state map that visually represents the existing workflow of the manufacturing process from start to finish. A future state map is created to represent how value will flow in an improved process, where non-value-adding activities are eliminated and optimized value adding activities are drawn. Value stream mapping is often referred to as VSM.

Usually, value stream maps are read from right to left.

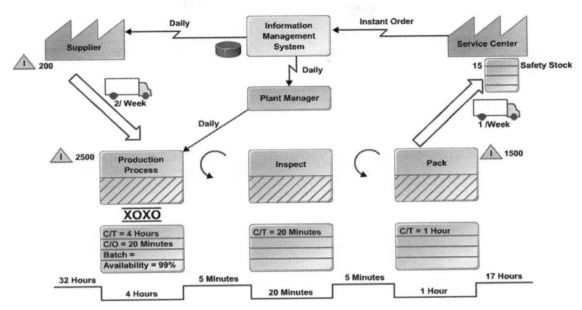

Fig: Example of value stream mapping

What is the difference between Current State & Future State Value Stream Maps?

Current State Value Stream Maps - A current state value stream map shows business processes as they currently exist. It helps identify areas where wastes occur and opportunities for improvement exist.

Future State Value Stream Maps - A future state value stream map shows improvements that need to be made in a value stream to eliminate waste in the process. It helps Lean teams in developing improvement strategies to be applied in their business processes.

Explain the concept of Kanban?

Lean organizations use visual inventory cues, such as Kanban, to pull the required amount of materials to produce a specific number of products at the right time.

Kanban can be either a card or a reusable container. Production line operators produce components when they receive a card or an empty container. An empty Kanban card indicates the need to produce parts, and in case there is a change in specifications, steps are taken to ensure that each line operator produces just enough and then stops.

Kanban differs from other inventory management and planning processes because production or component delivery is pulled through the production line, rather than against it, which is the push method. The push method is used in the traditional forecast-oriented manufacturing process.

What is Visual Factory?

In a Lean manufacturing process, time and resources spent on conveying data and information are regarded as waste. Visual factory tools—such as signs, charts, check sheets, and more—simplify information and reduce resources and time consumed to make it accessible. Clear and concise real-time information and feedback regarding the status of a plant or a process is provided to shop floor employees using visual cues and tools. The visual cues provide unambiguous information needed to perform their jobs at a glance. Simple visual cues—such as color-coded pipes, wires, or flags; painted floor areas; and indicator lights—are simple to use and understand. The type of tool and the location used are determined by identifying the relevance and the information recipient.

What is TPM?

Total Productive Maintenance (TPM) is a maintenance management system where every employee, from top management to the production equipment operator, maximizes the effectiveness of the production system by preventing accidents, defects, and breakdowns. TPM improves overall effectiveness by maximizing equipment effectiveness and establishing a system of *preventive maintenance (PM)* across the lifespan of a piece of equipment. TPM is by autonomous groups or individuals and by departments such as engineering, operations, and maintenance.

Narrate with an example the benefits of TPM?

A steel furniture manufacturer faced production losses and rejections because of the frequent breakdowns and feeding defects of an automated coil feed fabrication line. The manufacturer decided to implement TPM, and as a first step, a 15-member team was chosen for TPM training. After completing the training in spring, the team set about implementing TPM. The team discovered that although the automated coil feed fabrication line was supposed to run 90 percent of the time; 40 percent of the time was spent in idling, minor stoppages, breakdowns, setups, and adjustments. Upon completing the TPM project, daily maintenance and productive maintenance caught problems before they happened and reduced the emergency maintenance of the machine. Consequently, there was significant reduction in setup time, stoppages, and idling time.

The summary of the results is as follows:
- Overall equipment effectiveness up by 25-65 percent.
- Quality defects down by 25-50 percent.
- Maintenance expenditures down by 10-50 percent.
- And, percent planned versus unplanned maintenance increased by 10-60 percent.

What is PM (Preventive Maintenance)?

PM is a schedule of planned maintenance actions aimed at preventing machinery breakdowns and failures. The primary goal of preventive maintenance is to improve equipment reliability and prevent equipment failure by proactively replacing worn components before they fail.

Explain the term Standard Work that is used in Lean?

Standard work is the systematic method of identifying, improving, and standardizing the most efficient method for performing work in a Lean environment by using available resources, namely people, equipment, and materials. It provides the person performing a task the impetus to complete the task using the most efficient method every time without fail. Standard work assures predictability through reducing variations, and synchronizing various processes, and providing a baseline for continuous improvement. It also highlights the critical points in a process; defines operator procedures; and describes the production sequence, safety issues, and quality checks.

Share an example of standard work in an Automobile Manufacturing Plant?

Recently, there were complaints about defective parts produced by the crank shaft grinding department. Management concluded that the defects were due to the lack of a standardized work procedure. They identified a machine as a detection mechanism and used it to measure the parts as they were manufactured to find out whether they were within a given tolerance. The data collected by the detection mechanism was analysed and used as a starting point to establish standard work. All the line operators were instructed to follow the procedures set in the standard work manual. This resulted in a reduced number of defects. However, management continued using the detection machine to generate a new set of data and monitored the work for continual improvement of work procedures.

What are Value-Added Activities

A *value-added activity* is any activity that increases the worth of a product or service. It directly contributes to meeting customer requirements, and customers are willing to pay for it. Value-added activities also generate a positive ROI for an organization. Without these activities, the process will be affected. A lean team should analyze if activities in a process actually add value to a product or service. They should also determine if activities in a process can be performed in parallel or be merged. This will help organizations deliver outputs more efficiently.

Example: In a manufacturing process, value-added activities can include: receiving a part request, preparing an internal request for a part from production, finding a relevant plant for issuing a request, finding production availability, updating part request information, and the manager processing the part request information and updating the request.

What are Non-Value-Added Activities?

Non-value-added activities are activities that consume resources and time without adding any value to a service or product. Non-value-added activities do not contribute to customer satisfaction and, therefore, customers are not willing to pay for these activities. They are not important to the production and delivery of a product or service, and eliminating them will not affect a process. Because non-value-added activities do not generate any positive ROI but incur only expenditures, organizations should focus on eliminating them.

Example: In the manufacturing process, non-value-added activities can include: sorting and organizing requests, searching for relevant part production locations, checking locations for availability and delivery, generating production requests, and reviewing the status of requests.

What are types of wastes in processes?

Organizations strive to eliminate three basic categories of waste in their business processes.

Basic Waste Category are:
- **Wasteful activity** - Work that adds no value to a product or service. Eliminating such activities from business processes will help organizations cut cost.
- **Unevenness** - This denotes inconsistencies that exist in a business process. Unevenness and inconsistencies can be avoided by eliminating inventory and supplying items to the production process only when they are needed.
- **Overburden** - This is caused by an unreasonable or excessive strain on resources. It can be eliminated by simplifying and standardizing processes.

Among these three basic categories of wastes, Lean focuses on eliminating activities that do not add any value. These activities are further classified into seven types of wastes: transport, inventory, motion, waiting, overproduction, over processing, and defects.

What do you understand by Theory of Constraints (ToC)?

The *Theory of Constraints (TOC)* is a management approach to managing the weakest link in a process. A process can have one or more weak links, called constraints that can be anything that prevents the process from performing to its maximum potential. TOC contends that a few constraints control the performance of a process, and therefore provide a mixture of related processes and interrelated concepts to increase the throughput.

What do you mean by throughput and Drum-Buffer-Rope in TOC?

Throughput - Throughput is the rate at which a process generates money through sales, not through production.

Drum-Buffer-Rope - Drum-buffer-rope is a TOC production planning technique that maximizes the flow of materials in a plant for which there is an immediate customer demand.

What the 5 steps followed in theory of constraints approach?

Theory of constraints has five steps. They are;

1. **Identify the constraint** : The constraint must be identified before an attempt is made to improve the throughput.
2. **Exploit the constraint** : If a constraint is responsible for reducing the output, then it should be pushed to yield the maximum output.
3. **Subordinate to the constraint** : The rest of the process should provide maximum support to the constraint to maximize its throughput.
4. **Elevate the constraint** : Improve performance by adding more capacity by way of additional resources.
5. **Do not let inertia set in** : If the weak link has been strengthened, go back to step one and implement TOC on the new weakest link.

Can you give an example for how TOC can be used in real life?

An automobile manufacturer discovered that his die casting machines were manufacturing just 25 shots per hour against an industry average of 60 shots per hour. Management decided to make 60 shots per hour the goal and sets about to achieve this using the five focusing steps described by TOC. To identify the constraint, the "shot per hour data" was analysed. The data identified the second shift start-ups on Wednesday as the lowest shift and the die cast machines as the constraint resource. This made Wednesday's the lowest in terms of production and the highest in terms of scrap.

Management decided to increase the throughput on the constraint resource on Wednesday's. Once the constraint was identified, management decided to exploit the constraint. Stuck parts, operator absenteeism, and a lack of space in the trimming line were identified as some of the causes for low-producing start-ups. The solutions to these problems were:

1. Perform difficult start-up jobs at shut-down and when experienced operators can start them up on the second shift.
2. Have first shift operators cover for absent second shift operators.
3. Clear trim lines prior to shut down and ensure that the second shift has room in the trimming line.

Once the solutions were implemented, management conducted a process meeting on how to subordinate the constraint by giving the second shift start-ups full support in terms of resources. Simultaneously, an action plan was put in place and steps were taken to ensure that the second shift had extra machines and operators to increase productivity. The constraint was removed as evidenced by the fact that the second shift produced an average of 62 shots per hour against the 25 shots per hour before the start of the TOC project. This is a 60 percent improvement on start-ups, which indicates the process has succeeded in elevating the constraint. Because they succeeded in overcoming one constraint, management decided to focus on other constraints in the process and applied TOC to the next weakest link in the process. By turning their attention to the other constraints, they prevented inertia from setting in.

. . . . .

2 Introduction to DMAIC Methodology

You described the basic concepts related to Six Sigma. A Six Sigma organization must apply a methodology that matches its process requirements. In this topic, you will describe the Six Sigma Define, Measure, Analyze, Improve, and Control (DMAIC) methodology. An organization implementing a quality improvement approach must use the right methodology to produce the desired results. Different Six Sigma methodologies are designed to match the specific requirements of an organization. The DMAIC methodology is widely used by organizations for applying process improvement efforts in their existing business processes. By understanding the DMAIC methodology, you can implement Six Sigma to meet customer expectations and requirements.

DMAIC Methodology

The *DMAIC* methodology is a data-driven methodology that is widely adopted for improving existing processes in an organization. It is used by improvement teams to eliminate the causes of defects and is a crucial part of an organization's Six Sigma initiative. It is a process that consists of five interconnected phases that a Six Sigma organization is expected to follow. DMAIC, in fact, is an acronym of five phases, namely Define, Measure, Analyze, Improve, and Control.

- **Define** - This phase defines customer's requirement, problems or improvement opportunities, and processes to be improved are identified and defined. In addition, the purpose and scope of the projects are clearly stated.
- **Measure-** The performance of the business process is measured by collecting relevant data using statistical tools.
- **Analyze-** The data collected is analysed and root causes of problems and opportunities for improvement are determined. After comparing various options, top alternatives are chosen.
- **Improve-** Solutions that address the root causes of the problem are generated by the team. You will also conduct trials before you can arrive at the best solution.
- **Control-** The current processes are improved by applying solutions that address the root causes of the problem. Statistical Process Control (SPC) mechanisms are setup to track process deviations and recurrences of root causes in the future. Improvement benefits are computed and the project is formally signed-off and closed.

Share an example of application of DMAIC methodology from software industry.

Applying the DMAIC Methodology in a Software Product Development Company.

In the Define phase, the Six Sigma team in a software product development company found that customers identified many issues in the beta version of its software.

However, if all the issues raised were to be fixed, timelines would slip and the budget would increase. The team then calculated the number of changes and the time and budget required for fixing these issues in the Measure phase.

In the Analyze phase, the team determined if the changes were aligned with the scope of the project and then identified changes that should be made. It also identified conflicting changes pointed out by the reviewers, communication gaps between the developers and the customers, and ways in which changes were communicated to the developers as other major causes of the issues.

In the Improve phase, the Six Sigma team took several steps, such as determining the limitations of the software, having regular meetings with customers, identifying the appropriate application to communicate the changes to the developers, creating change requests, and monitoring the implementation of the approved changes until closure to eliminate the issues.

Finally, appropriate mechanisms were set up in the Control phase to monitor the regularity of meetings and communication between the developers and customers as well as to monitor the performance and usage of the change request feature.

What are the advantages of the DMAIC Methodology?

The DMAIC methodology has some distinct advantages and may prove beneficial to any organization implementing it. This methodology:

- Focuses on satisfying both internal and external customers.
- Analyzes problems thoroughly.
- Validates the root cause of the problems using accurate data.
- Substantiates the impact of the methodology through the results measured.
- And, strives to maintain the gains and sustain the improvements made.

■ ■ ■ ■ ■

Introduction to the DFSS Methodology

In the previous topic, you described the basic concepts related to the DMAIC methodology. Design for Six Sigma (DFSS) is another popular methodology adopted to implement Six Sigma in new business processes in an organization. In this topic, you will describe the DFSS methodology.

Any organization deploying a Six Sigma project should determine whether the right methodology is selected for implementation. While implementing Six Sigma in new business processes, organizations need to use the DFSS methodology. Knowledge of the DFSS approach enables you to properly implement Six Sigma through the DFSS methodology and improve the business performance of new processes.

What is DFSS?

Design for Six Sigma (DFSS) is a quality improvement approach that organizations use for designing new products, processes, and services that meet Six Sigma quality levels. Because nearly 40 percent of sales and 50 percent of profits of most growing organizations come from new products, it is imperative for organizations to launch new products. DFSS is used not only for designing new products, processes, and services, but also for redesigning existing products, processes, and services. Nearly 70 to 80 percent of quality-related problems in companies are linked to product design. To address this problem and to bring order to product design, companies adopt the DFSS approach. The DFSS approach includes a roadmap, specific tools, metrics, and a training program. The main focus of DFSS is to implement the Six Sigma methodology at the earliest possible moment in the product or service life cycle.

Explain with an example, the application of DFSS methodology?

A washing machine manufacturer decided to design a low-cost braking system for domestic washing machines with an improved level of braking performance and life. The principles of DFSS, including the application of robust design concepts such as DOE, simulation methods such as Monte Carlo simulation, and tolerance design were used to design the new braking system. The old braking system would brake within seven seconds of application, and management wanted to design a new braking system that would brake within three seconds and at a cost lower by 30 percent. Customer and process requirements were identified using different methods and the transfer function of $Y = f(X)$ was constructed based on several rounds of DOE and tolerance design. The Monte Carlo simulation technique was also used to predict the failure rate of the proposed design and its performance pattern.

While designing a new product, several DFSS tools including robust design concepts and simulation methods are used.

DFSS Tool	Description
Design of Experiments (DOE)	<ul><li>Identifies varying levels of independent variables in a process.</li><li>Brings out the cause-and-effect relationship among different factors.</li><li>Can result in significant improvements to products and processes.</li></ul>
Monte Carlo simulation	<ul><li>Provides the most likely outcomes.</li><li>Calculates a range of possible results.</li><li>Well suited for complex projects.</li></ul>
Tolerance design	<ul><li>Involves experiments to predict the effects of tolerances, which are measurement values that determine if a product or service is</li></ul>

	acceptable or unacceptable to customers.
	• Ensures that all tolerances have the maximum effect.
	• Modifies the tolerances to optimize the design.

What is Design of Experiments (DOE)?

It is a technique used to systematically identify varying levels of independent variables in a process to ensure that the outcome is beneficial to the improvement of the entire process. Generally, DOE brings out the cause-and-effect relationship among different factors that affect the process output. When done properly, DOE can result insignificant improvements to products and processes, including shorter development cycles, more robust products, and cost reductions.

Example: The output of a nuclear reactor in this new design needs to be substantially higher than other reactors. Therefore, a DOE is conducted to find out the factors that impact the output of the nuclear reactor. The output being considered in this case is yield. It is the "percentage of nuclear material reacted upon" during the nuclear Reaction. Experts short listed five factors, namely feed rate (litres/minute), catalyst (%), agitation rate (rotations per minute [RPM]), temperature (degree Fahrenheit), and concentration (%) as factors which will impact the yield. The output of the experiment will include 16 readings from which significant factors can be identified.

What is Monte Carlo simulation?

It is a technique that provides Six Sigma teams with the most likely outcomes and the relevant consequences of choosing a certain plan of action. Besides the what-if scenario analysis method, this is the other most common simulation type. This analysis does not produce a single result, but calculates a range of possible results. It has a wide range of applications in many fields, including finance and engineering. Because it works effectively with large quantities of numbers, it is well suited for complex projects in which more than a few inputs, such as cost, activity, and duration, are unknown.

Example: An automobile manufacturer decided to use the Monte Carlo simulation technique to predict the variation in the braking performance of a braking assembly for an automobile. The variation in performance occurs due to variation in several input factors such as moisture, the condition of sub-assembly components, and material variations. By feeding the distributions of input factor variations to the statistical model obtained from hypothesis testing and experiments, the simulated output in braking performance was produced.

What is Tolerance design?

It involves experiments that are carried out to predict the effects of tolerances, which are measurement values that determine if a product or service is acceptable or unacceptable to customers. Tolerances are the permissible limits of variation in a process against which data collected will be analysed. They are typically expressed in ranges. If the result of a test falls within the range specified by the tolerance, it is acceptable. If not, it is considered unacceptable. Tolerance design is conducted to ensure that all tolerances have the maximum effect and to modify the tolerances to optimize the design.

Example: A manufacturer uses tolerance design to design a caliper assembly. The different components of the assembly, such as the piston, caliper, cylinder, seals, pads, rotor, and cylinder cover have variations in dimensions because of their manufacturing processes. To establish tolerances for each of these components, worst case scenarios are traditionally used. But in the DFSS approach, tolerances are computed while keeping in mind the variation of components and the functional requirement of the caliper assembly.

What are Stage Gates? And how it is relevant in product development?

It is a technique used by companies to screen and pass projects as they progress through different development stages. In this technique, the development process is divided into different stages, which are separated by gates. At each gate, there is a review of the particular stage of the development process to determine the continuation of the development process. A robust new product development process includes these stage gates:

- Concept study
- Feasibility investigations
- Development of new products
- Maintenance
- And, continuous learning

DFSS and Stage Gates

DFSS and stage gates are among the widely used new product development (NPD) strategies. Many companies integrate DFSS with existing stage gates during new product development processes. The stage gates for DFSS projects are either at the Identify, Design, Optimize, and Validate (IDOV) or the Define, Measure, Analyze, Design, and Verify (DMADV) phases.

What are the different roadmaps available for implementing DFSS approach?

Organizations use different roadmaps to implement the DFSS approach to deliver products and services that meet customer requirements.

Roadmap	Description
IDOV	• Focuses on bringing continuous improvement to the product design process. • Consists of four phases, namely Identify, Define, Optimize, and

	validate.
DMADV	• Implements Six Sigma projects involved in designing new products and services. • Consists of five phases called Define, Measure, Analyze, Design, and Verify.
Systematic design	• A design process that takes into account the environment and other systems related to the problem.
French design	• Helps reduce the steps involved in the design process. • Approaches a problem in diverse ways. • Generates innovative steps and design philosophies to address a problem.

Explain IDOV roadmap of DFSS approach?

Phase	Description
Identify	• Voice of the customer is gathered and converted into technical requirements. • A business case is established and a project charter is prepared. • A team is formed and roles and responsibilities are set.
Design	• Concept design is developed. • Risks associated with the chosen concept design are also determined. • The functional requirements and their CTQ attributes are identified and deployed. • Sigma capability is predicted.
Optimize	• Capability of the process is evaluated. • Design is optimized for reliability and performance.
Validate	• Prototype is tested using formal tools to validate the design. • New requirements to be met are sent to manufacturing and sourcing units. • Design is iterated. • A final phase review is done.

Identify
The voice of the customer (VOC) is gathered and converted into technical requirements in this phase. A business case is then established and a project charter is prepared along with milestones. A team is also formed to carry out the project. Roles and responsibilities of the team members are also set during this phase. These activities are accomplished using tools such as Quality Function Deployment (QFD); Failure Modes and Effects Analysis (FMEA); the Suppliers,

Inputs, Process, Outputs, and Customers (SIPOC) diagram; the Integrated Product Delivery System (IDPS); target costing; and benchmarking.

Design

In this phase, the concept design is developed by formulating alternative concepts and choosing the best concept after evaluating the alternatives. Risks associated with the chosen concept design are also determined. The functional requirements and their Critical to Quality (CTQ) attributes are identified by the Six Sigma team. The CTQ attributes are deployed after assessing their effect on functional requirements. Raw materials and their procurement plan with the related manufacturing plan are created during this phase. In addition, the Sigma capability is predicted. These activities are accomplished using tools such as smart simple design, risk assessment, FMEA, engineering analysis, materials selection software, simulation, DOE, systems engineering, and the capability of the process is evaluated to verify if the CTQs can be met.

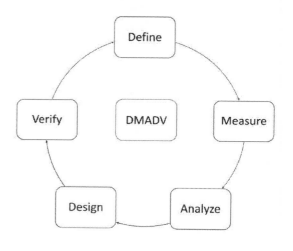

Fig: DMADV

Optimize

The design is optimized for reliability and performance by developing detailed design elements. This helps optimize the Sigma capability and cost. These activities are accomplished through manufacturing database and flow back tools, a design for manufacturability, process capability models, a robust design, Monte Carlo methods, tolerancing, and Six Sigma tools.

Validate

The prototype is tested using formal tools to validate the design. After evaluating the performance, failure modes, and risks of the design, new requirements to be met are sent to manufacturing and sourcing units. The design is iterated until it meets the requirements of the customer. A final phase review to assess the reliability is also carried out to validate the design. The term Verify is also used interchangeably for this phase. These activities are accomplished through accelerated testing, reliability engineering, FMEA, and disciplined New Product Introduction (NPI).

Share an example for using IDOV to Implement DFSS?

A washing machine manufacturer decided to use the IDOV roadmap to adopt the DFSS approach for designing a low-cost braking system for domestic washing machines with an improved level of braking performance and life. In the Identify phase, customer needs, reliability, cost, quality, and technology requirements were identified and prioritized.

In the Design phase, the transfer function for the braking system Y = f(X) was generated and validated. A design feasibility study was also conducted. Then, vendors for components were selected.

In the Optimize phase, the braking system's cycle time of 39 seconds in the prototype was optimized to 3 seconds through a series of experiments. Moreover, tolerances for subsystems were specified and the process capability was demonstrated.

Finally, in the Validate phase, the operations were scaled up for production, mistake proofing was done, and the equipment was tested. The company also gained the approval of its customers in this phase of the IDOV process.

Explain DMADV Methodology?

Another roadmap of DFSS is *DMADV,* an acronym for five interconnected phases, namely Define, Measure, Analyze, Design, and Verify. This methodology is used in projects that involve creating a new product or process design.

Define - The project goals are defined so that they are in line with customer requirements and enterprise strategies.

Measure - Characteristics that are critical to quality as well as product and process capabilities are measured.

Analyze - The different process options are analysed and the best process that is consistent with customer requirements is selected.

Design - The details of the process are designed and optimized to meet the needs of customers followed by the performance of the new design which is tested through pilot runs before implementation.

Verify – In this phase the results are test and implementation of new design is carried out for large scale deployment.

How to apply DMADV Methodology in IT industry? Explain with an example?

A sports apparel company decided to launch a website to increase its sales through online marketing.

In the Define phase, the Six Sigma team formulates a goal of designing of a user friendly website that would be listed in the top 10 search results on all major search engines.

In the Measure phase, the popularity of different keywords and the ranking of the keywords in the search engines are measured.

In the Analyze phase, the keywords that needed to be used in the website are chosen after examining the collected keyword ranking data. In addition, different search engine optimization techniques, such as directories to which the website must be submitted and websites to which links must be given and analysed.

In the Design phase, the most user-friendly site design is selected from three different website designs that are created. The keywords that were short listed should be plugged into the website. Back links are also given to appropriate websites, and the website should be submitted to top directories.

In the Verify phase, the ability of the website to generate traffic will be checked through periodic reports from web traffic analysis tools on the ranking of the keywords and the number of visitors routed to the website.

What are the readiness points for DFSS Deployment?

Before deploying DFSS, the readiness of an organization to deploy DFSS must be assessed. The factors that indicate an organization's readiness to deploy DFSS include:

- Steadily increasing Sigma levels.
- A written schedule of prioritized project ideas.
- Awareness of changes in the market and customer requirements.
- And, the ability to gauge the organization's capability for success with DFSS.

What are the differences between DFSS and DMAIC?

DFSS and DMAIC are two of the methodologies commonly used by organizations to implement. Six Sigma. Organizations with well-developed Six Sigma programs also run DMAIC and DFSS projects concurrently.

Feature	Description
Focus	• DMAIC: Improving the existing products and services or processes. • DFSS: Developing new products and services or processes or redesigning them.
Nature of the project	• DMAIC: Projects are easier and faster and provide early gains. • DFSS: Projects take longer to implement and benefits are visible only in the long run.
Process	• DMAIC: Projects are related to manufacturing, transactional processes, or enabling processes. • DFSS: Projects also include product design.

. . . .

Quality Function Deployment

In the previous topic, you described the DFSS methodology used to implement Six Sigma. Improving customer satisfaction is one of the major goals of a Six Sigma project. One of the methods used for translating customer requirements into technical requirements in QFD.

In this topic, you will describe QFD. One of the major challenges of a Six Sigma program is to convert the needs of customers into technical requirements to ensure that your Six Sigma effort meets customer requirements. QFD is a method that enables you to convert customer requirements into technical requirements.

An understanding of QFD and its subsequent implementation helps ensure that the Six Sigma project in your organization enhances customer satisfaction.

What is the definition of QFD?

Quality Function Deployment (QFD) is a structured approach followed by customer-driven organizations to transform customer requirements into their product specifications.

The QFD process begins with the identification of customer requirements and the goals of the QFD team. It is here where product or service characteristics desired by customers are identified. These characteristics are called the "**what's**."

Then, the ways and means of achieving these characteristics, or "whats," are identified. These methods are called the "**how's**." This process is applied in each phase of the development cycle.

Thus, QFD provides an insight into the whole design of a product, thereby eliminating production problems that may arise during manufacturing.

The QFD approach involves four phases and each phase uses a series of matrices to collect information and develop a plan for the product.

QFD Phase	Description
Product planning or House of Quality (HOQ)	• Customer requirements and market opportunities are translated into technical requirements. Organizations: • Define and prioritize customer requirements. • Analyze competitive opportunities. • Plan a product in response. • Establish the critical characteristic target values.
Product design	• Technical requirements of the product are translated into critical characteristics. Organizations: • Identify the critical parts and assemblies.

	• Flow them down. • Translate them into assembly characteristics and target values.

Process planning or process design	• Critical operations for achieving critical part characteristics are identified. Organizations:
	   ○ Determine the critical processes and their flow.
	   ○ Develop production equipment requirements.
	   ○ Establish critical or key parameters for the process.

Production planning or process control	• Process control, quality control plans, maintenance, and training plans are established. Organizations: • Establish various methods for controlling the process.

What do you know about Yoji Akao's Quality Approach?

Based on QFD, Yoji Akao, a Japanese planning specialist who developed QFD, developed a quality approach for products that involves the following steps:

1. Conduct surveys on quality demands from customers in your target market. This will help you determine the important characteristics of your product in the market.
2. Study other important characteristics of the market and create a demand quality deployment chart that reflects the market's demands and characteristics.
3. Analyze competitive products in the market through competitive analysis. Based on this, develop a quality plan and determine the selling features of your product.
4. Determine the level of importance for each of the quality demands of your product.
5. List the elements of quality and develop a quality elements deployment chart.
6. Combine the demand quality deployment chart and the quality elements deployment chart to make a quality chart of your product.
7. Analyze competitors' products to see how they perform with respect to these quality elements.
8. Analyze customer complaints to check for quality elements.
9. Determine the most important quality elements for your products based on customer complaints and quality demands.
10. Create a specific design quality after studying the quality characteristics and converting them into quality elements.
11. Establish the quality assurance method and other test methods for your product.

What to you understand by House of Quality (HOQ)?

The *House of Quality (HOQ)* is a diagram used by a product development team during the initial stage of the QFD process. It uses a planning matrix to define the relationship between customer requirements and the capability of the product and the company to satisfy these requirements. Because this matrix looks like a house, where customer requirements and product attributes resemble the main living quarters, competitive analysis resembles the porch, and the correlation matrix resembles the roof, it is called **House of Quality.**

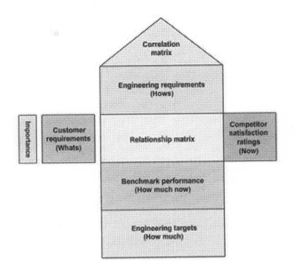

Fig: House of Quality (HOQ)

What are the different elements of QFD?

HOQ encompasses different QFD elements used for understanding customer requirements and aligning business processes to meet these customer requirements.

QFD Element	Description
Customer requirements	• Gathered using tools such as focus groups, surveys, and customer experiences. • A structured list of customer requirements is drawn using tools such as affinity diagrams and tree diagrams.
Importance ratings	• Customer requirements are quantified and rated according to their importance on a scale of 1 to 5.
Competitive analysis	• Customer views about competitors' products or services are gathered through research.
Technical requirements	• Technical requirements not known to customers are identified and documented.
Relationship matrix	• The relationship between customer requirements and an organization's ability to meet those requirements is determined.
Importance weighting rating	• Customer requirements are weighted according to their importance to prioritize key criteria.

Target values	• Service attributes or technical descriptors that can be used as benchmarks against competitors' target values are established.
Engineering analysis	• Technical descriptors are compared with the competitors' technical descriptors using scientific analytical techniques.
Correlation matrix	• Relationships among customer requirements are analysed to identify correlated requirements.

It starts with **customer requirements.** The customers for a product or service are identified and their requirements from the product or service are gathered using different tools such as focus groups, surveys, and customer experiences. A structured list of customer requirements is then drawn by analysing and organizing this data using tools such as affinity diagrams and tree diagrams.

Importance ratings are used for quantify the customer requirements and rated according to their importance on a scale of 1 to 5. This rating will be used in the relationship matrix at a later stage.

Another element is the **Competitive analysis** where customer's views about the competition are gathered through research to provide a better understanding of the market. Here, the customers rate an organization's products or services against competitors' products or services. Also, **Technical requirements** that are not known to customers are identified and documented. These requirements generally stem from management or regulatory standards that a product must meet.

Relationship matrix defines the relationship between customer requirements and an organization's ability to meet those requirements is determined. The relationship between the two factors is classified as weak, moderate, or strong and given the values of 1, 3, and 9, respectively. Even, in **Importance weighting rating**, Customer requirements are weighted according to their importance for defining and prioritizing key criteria. The relative importance of customer needs and the company's and competitor's performance are taken into account while calculating this. **Target values** for each product or service attributes, known as technical descriptors, that can be used as benchmarks against competitors' target values are established. These target values are the "how much" of these product or service attributes.

The technical descriptors are compared with the competitors' technical descriptors using scientific analytical techniques to assess their properties is called **Engineering analysis.** This also includes reverse engineering competitors' products or services to determine the values for their technical descriptors. **Correlation matrix** is the relationship among customer requirements are analysed to identify correlated requirements. The relationships are then ranked for determining areas of improvement that need to be focused upon.

How QFD assesses the value for product and service offering characteristics?

QFD focuses on fixing customer value to an organization's product or service. There are two types of value characteristics:

- **Product value characteristics:** They include performance, functionality, usability, simplicity of design, benefits corresponding to cost, durability, safety, availability, and serviceability.
- **Service value characteristics:** They include competence, understanding customers' needs, responsiveness, timeliness, accuracy, reliability, confidentiality, credibility, access, and communication.

Why should an organization consider using QFD?

QFD offers several benefits to organizations.

- It reduces design cycle time due to the decrease in design changes.
- It reduces the overall product development time because the focus is solely on satisfying key customer needs.
- It reduces overall cost by reducing design changes.
- It improves customer satisfaction because the development process is driven by the voice of the customer (VOC).
- It rates a product against other products in the market through competitor analysis.
- And, it documents identified competitive marketing strategies.

■ ■ ■ ■ ■

3 Define Phase

In this lesson, you will describe the fundamentals of the Define phase. Before you can begin with the activities in this phase, it is helpful to start with a basic understanding of the purpose of the phase, the activities that take place within it and its tools and deliverables. Identifying and defining customer requirements and problem areas in a process are difficult without appropriate tools.

Six Sigma uses a number of tools that help you pinpoint customer requirements and problem areas. An understanding of the different tools and deliverables used by Six Sigma practitioners will help you apply the tools and generate the desired deliverables.

The Define Phase

In the Define phase of the DMAIC methodology, problems or improvement opportunities and processes to be improved are identified and defined. The key activities that occur in the Define phase of the DMAIC methodology include:

- Developing a project charter that includes the business case, problem statement, and scope of the project, project objectives, team members, project schedule, and potential benefits.
- Identifying the Critical to Quality (CTQ) characteristics of your project.
- Selecting Six Sigma team members and obtaining authorization from the Six Sigma sponsor.
- Assembling Six Sigma team members and providing them with adequate training.
- And, building a high-level process map for the entire process.

What are tools used in Define Phase?

A Six Sigma team uses a number of tools in the Define phase to identify and define problem areas or opportunities for improvement. The tools include:

- **Project charter** is a document that provides a clear, concise description of the business needs that a project is intended to address. It not only makes a project official, but also gives Yellow Belts, Green Belts, or Black Belts the authority to lead the project and draw on organizational resources as needed. The project charter documents the expected results.
- **SIPOC** diagram is a high-level process map that is used to identify and define all the relevant elements that are necessary for improving a process before actual work begins. It is an acronym of these elements: Suppliers, Inputs, Processes, Outputs, and Customers. The SIPOC diagram helps process improvement teams understand the purpose and the scope of a process before they begin to measure or improve it. It is also called COPIS to emphasize that the entire process starts with customers. COPIS is an acronym of Customers, Outputs, Processes, Inputs, and Suppliers.

- **Affinity diagram** is a diagram that is used to organize different ideas that are generated in brainstorming sessions into meaningful groups.
- **Multi-Generational Planning (MGP)** is an approach that breaks projects into manageable phases. Each phase is called a generation, and therefore the approach is called MGP. Breaking down projects logically and rolling them out in a phased manner helps the process development team envision the various stages of a product or service. In the evolution of products or services, different functionalities are added several times in each phase of MGP. MGP helps you manage project scopes better in process improvement projects.
- **Stakeholder analysis** is an analysis used by quality improvement teams for identifying and evaluating people who will influence the outcome of a project to ensure that their interests are addressed. Knowing the effect that stakeholders will have on a project also helps in anticipating potential problems and devising strategies to handle them effectively.
- **Communication plan** is a written document that describes how different stakeholders and interested parties will be informed about the objectives of a project, the means of accomplishing these objectives, the tools to be used, improvements, solutions and how they impact stakeholders, project benefits, progress made, and the timeline.
- **VOC analysis** is used to understand customer requirements so that an organization can provide products and services that meet these requirements. It delivers products and services that satisfy customers that help organizations survive in a highly competitive market.
- **Kano analysis** is an analysis that measures the extent to which a product or service satisfies the requirements and expectations of customers. In other words, it defines the customers' requirement priorities. Professor Noriaki Kano developed Kano analysis, as it was named after him. The Kano model classifies product attributes based on how they are perceived by customers. It classifies customer requirements as mandatory requirements and delights. These classifications are useful for a customer-driven organization to make design decisions on its product.
- **Quality Function Deployment (QFD)** is a structured approach followed by customer-driven organizations to transform customer requirements into product specifications. QFD provides an insight into the whole design of a product, thereby eliminating production problems that may arise during manufacturing.
- **RACI matrix** is a tool used for clarifying roles, responsibilities, and authority in teams involved in a business process task. RACI is an acronym of the four responsibilities used, namely Responsible, Accountable, Consulted, and Informed.
- **Project prioritization matrix** is a tool used during brainstorming sessions for evaluating various issues against different criteria and prioritizing the issues. This helps identify issues that must be solved first to eliminate problems and improve processes.
- **Pareto chart** is a bar chart that displays various categories of problems in a project by the frequency of their occurrence. It is named after its creator, Vilfredo Pareto, a 19th

century economist. The objective of using a Pareto chart is to narrow down the primary causes of problems and focus efforts on tackling the most important causes. The Pareto chart is also known as the 80-20 chart.

These tools are used during the Define phase to understand selected projects better.

What are Define Phase Deliverables?

The main objective of the Define phase is to identify and state problem areas or opportunities for improvement. Customer requirements and existing performance metrics are collected to select the process that needs to be improved. The process chosen for improvement is the output of the Define phase.

·····

Process Elements

One of the important activities of the Define phase is to define problems and improvement opportunities in a process. To successfully perform these tasks, it is essential for you to have basic knowledge about how processes are demarcated in terms of their execution across several functions.

What do you understand by Functional Boundaries?

Most conventional organizations comprise departments and functions. A department head or functional head is responsible for all department deliverables. All department members should have clearly defined responsibilities for their respective tasks. Departmental tasks are expected to be performed on time and with quality. Every member of a department operates within a framework called a functional silo.

Functional silos focus on their own objectives alone and are not involved in interacting with other groups and sharing internal process information with others. Each department may also have several cross-departmental tasks that fall outside of the functional silo. Cross-departmental tasks can have delivery and quality issues. The boundary set up between functional and cross-departmental tasks brings about key challenges, including:

- Layers of bureaucracy that involve too many approvals.
- Lack of ownership in cross-departmental tasks.
- Management frustration due to lack of coordination among departments.
- Too many steps, such as checking and quality control, which are redundant for every department.
- Lack of focus on customers due to employee attention on internal tasks.
- And, opportunities for errors or corruption because of lack of ownership.

Example of Functional Boundaries: A truck manufacturer.

A truck manufacturer is developing a new cost-effective, low-horsepower truck. This conventional manufacturer is organized by departments. The research and development (R&D)

department develops the product based on requirements submitted by the marketing department. There is not much interaction or collaboration between these departments. The marketing department only signs off on the final prototype. By then, there is not much scope for the R&D team to accept changes and suggestions from the marketing department. The situation with the manufacturing and purchase departments is also similar. The components of the truck are not designed to suit the existing machinery or vendor capabilities.

As a result, procuring new machinery and identifying new vendors takes a long time, which is much longer than the actual project schedule. Because all the departments are organized by their respective functions, they strictly adhere to their functional boundaries. Therefore, the flow of information among various functions is restricted.

What are Cross-Functional Processes?

Cross-functional processes relate to a series of activities that are executed across an organization. Cross-functional processes are not organized by departments or functions, but by processes which comprise several departmental activities. In addition, cross-functional processes help clarify the end-to-end execution of a process. A cross-functional structure is a Six Sigma way of thinking how processes are structured and resources are aligned per key outputs. Therefore, a cross-functional structure facilitates better alignment to customer needs. Some of the benefits of a cross-functional process include:

- It becomes easy for top management to clarify its quality, cost, and delivery goals and deploy them to employees at every level.
- And, it facilitates close coordination among different departments in the organization.

Example of a Cross-Functional Process

Based on suggestions provided by a leading management consultant, the CEO of the truck manufacturing firm reorganized the entire organization by processes. New product development is one of the organization's processes, and this process had a diverse cross-functional team consisting of R&D, marketing, sales, supply chain, manufacturing, finance, HR, and quality team members. For each new model that the truck manufacturer wants to develop, a cross-functional team have to be formed. The members of the team have to be empowered to make their own decisions. This drastically reduces the lead time for the development of designs, components, and finished products.

As a result, products are delivered within the planned time. Also, due to constant feedback from the marketing, manufacturing, quality, and purchasing department team members, the new model matched what customers want. The formation of a cross-functional structure will effectively help the organization reposition itself in the market.

. . . . .

Identify Stakeholders and Process Owners

This step will help you identify process owners and key stakeholders who are involved in the process. Any process being executed will involve the participation of several key stakeholders and process owners.

When executing the Define phase of the DMAIC methodology, your role as a Six Sigma Green Belt involved determining all stakeholders involved in a process. By identifying their roles and responsibilities will help you accurately plan your strategies when defining problems and improvement opportunities in the process.

Define Stakeholders? And explain with an example?

A *stakeholder* is a person who has a business interest in the outcome of a project or who is actively involved in its work. Stakeholders take on various roles and responsibilities; their participation in the project will have an impact on its outcome and its chances for success.

Stakeholders may have competing interests, needs, priorities, and opinions. They may have conflicting visions for the project's successful outcome. You must identify the internal and external stakeholders as early as possible, learn what their needs are, and secure their participation in defining the project's parameters and success criteria. While it may be difficult to negotiate to a consensus early in the project, it is far less painful and costly than getting to the end of the project only to learn that someone's needs were not met or were misunderstood.

Example: Stakeholders of a Solar Car Project.
An automobile company decided to start a solar car plant in a new location. The stakeholders for the project include the project manager, project sponsor, government automobile regulatory agency officials, company staff and employees, management, the production team, the company's vendors, local environmental and political groups, and nearby residents.

Some of their responsibilities of stakeholders include:
- Consumers of products or services.
- Beneficiaries of any improvement in the product or service as a result of a Green Belt project.

Who are Sponsors in Six Sigma projects?

Sponsors may be individuals or groups who are usually process owners or business owners and are willing to provide financial assistance to the project. The responsibilities of a sponsor include:
- Facilitating financial resources for the project.
- Signing and publishing the project charter.
- Having ultimate accountability for the success of the project.
- Signing off on all planning documents and change requests.

- Authorizing teams to use resources.
- Championing and supporting the project manager and team.
- Clearing roadblocks and challenges faced by the project team.
- Reviewing progress and quality.
- Cutting through red tape and expediting activities.

What is a Project steering committee?

The project steering committee is also known as quality council. Executives in the steering committee are a part of the project selection committees and belong to the high-level project governance side of the organization. Their review considerations may include:
- Gauging the Return on Investment (ROI) of the project.
- Identifying the value of the project.
- Analysing the risks involved in taking up the project.
- Identifying the factors that may influence the project.

Who are Process Owners & what is there role in Six Sigma projects?

A *process owner* is a person who has the ultimate accountability for the output of a process. The process owner is also accountable for the timely delivery of deliverables, their quality, and any other attributes critical to the process such as cost, utilization, and productivity. The process owner approves various documents that are required to support the entire process. The process owner is also responsible for the workflow coordination and management at every stage of the process.

With the help of a process improvement team, the process owner ensures a high-performance process in the organization. Incidentally, the process owner is the only person who has the authority to make any changes to the process and make decisions for process improvements.

Example: The Process Owner in a Memory Chip Manufacturing Company.
Janrex Inc., a leading memory chip manufacturing company for nearly a decade, was facing a decline in its annual sales for the past two years. Faced with stiff competition in the industry, the company was under considerable pressure to maintain its position as a market leader.

The organization formed a Six Sigma team and gave it the responsibility of selecting appropriate projects where Six Sigma could be successfully deployed. Before selecting Six Sigma projects, management identified the head of the supply chain department, the Senior Vice President (SVP), as the process owner in the organization because the SVP was responsible for approving various documents required to support the entire process.

How to Identify Stakeholders and Process Owners?

It is important to identify stakeholders early in the project; analyze relevant information regarding their interests, expectations, importance, and influence; and devise a strategy to ensure their involvement to maximize positive influences and mitigate potential negative impacts.

Guidelines

To identify project stakeholders and process owners, follow these guidelines:

- Perform a review of project and related information to create the list of internal and external parties who may be impacted by the project. The documents or information that are valuable sources for stakeholder identification include:
    o The project charter.
    o Procurement documents.
    o The organization or company structure.
    o The organization or company culture.
    o Government or industry standards.
    o Stakeholder register templates.
    o Lessons learned from previous projects.
    o Stakeholder registers from previous projects.
- Write down all the names of interest groups, departments, individuals, teams, and authorities, who are:
    o Concerned in any way with the project.
    o Located in the plant or geographic region of impact.
    o Holding influential positions.
    o Owners of the performance outcome of the process, which provides inputs to the process being improved.
    o Affected by the problems addressed in the project.
- Classify the people who are directly involved or indirectly involved in your project's life cycle.
- Identify the process owner who is accountable for the timely delivery of deliverables, their quality, and any other attributes critical to the process.

Example: Identifying Stakeholders and Process Owners in a Six Sigma Project.

A computer manufacturer wants to improve the on-time delivery percentage of finished goods from 75 percent to 95 percent. The SVP of the supply chain, the process owner, has commissioned this improvement project.

As part of Six Sigma implementation, the SVP identifies various stakeholders in the entire manufacturing process. Here, the stakeholders are dealers and resellers who buy the finished goods from the organization and then sell the goods to consumers. The supply chain department is responsible for the on-time delivery of finished goods to dealers and resellers. The supply chain department coordinates the requirement from sales, devising the monthly material requirement plan (MRP) for raw materials and finished goods. The MRP is subsequently helps us to find how to identify Stakeholders and Process Owners are deployed to production and vendors.

Internal logistics partners coordinate moving the raw materials from vendors' facilities to the manufacturing plant, while external logistics partners manage the movement of finished goods from the manufacturing plant to dealers. The manufacturing plant consists of production units, stores, quality control, maintenance, finance, HR, technology, and administration.

■ ■ ■ ■ ■

Identify Customers

You are familiar with the roles and responsibilities of stakeholders and process owners in a process. As projects and services are targeted toward customers, it is also essential for you to know about them. In this topic, you will identify the customers for a project. Executing a project successfully requires identifying the needs and expectations of your customers. Any impact on projects or processes will directly or indirectly influence customers. Having a thorough knowledge about customers will help you determine the impact of projects on customers and help you plan appropriately.

What is the difference between Internal Customers & External Customers?

Key differences between internal customers and external customers include:
- Internal customers are employees or others within an organization that is affected by a product or service. In addition, for every feeding process, its receiving process is an internal customer. External customers are end users such as clients and intermediate customers such as dealers, distributors, and regulators.
- Internal customers act as intermediaries, while external customers are the real customers of a final product or service.
- Also, internal customers do not always know the exact requirements, while external customers always know their requirements.

In which areas can we Six Sigma projects impact customers?

Six Sigma projects can have an impact on customers through:
- Striving for increased customer satisfaction.
- Reducing the number of defects and related anxiety.
- Providing reliable products.
- Offering lower prices for products or services.
- Offering a greater variety of products.
- Providing a positive impact on client processes and business for business-to-business (B2B) suppliers.

- Rising the trust level customers have in suppliers by providing more consistent supplier processes.
- And, striving for a positive impact on the environment.

How to Identify Customers?

Customers, both internal and external, play an important role in an organization's Six Sigma implementation.

To identify internal customers, follow these guidelines:
- Within the organization, identify departments, groups, teams, processes, and individuals who receive desired and undesired outputs of the process as their inputs.
- Consider outputs such as work-in-progress products, raw materials, information, and enabling tools. Internal customers are identified for entire processes within an organization, and not for an end product or a service.
- Identify the recipients of the primary output of the process or work-in-progress product, because they are the most important internal customers.

To identify external customers, follow these guidelines:
- Identify if the business end product or service reaches other businesses (B2B) or consumers (business-to-consumers [B2C]). In other words, determine organizations or individuals who purchase the product or service.
- In the case of B2B customers, you can pinpoint the organizations that are customers. You do not need to identify individuals in those customer organizations.
- In the case of B2C customers, it is very difficult to identify all the individual customers because of the size of the consumer base. Instead, identify customers as segments or groups, primarily classified by demography.
- Write down all the names of groups, industries, organizations, and individual business owners who are end users of the product or service.
- Write down all the names of groups, industries, organizations, and individual business owners who are intermediate customers such as resellers and dealers.
- Write down all the names of groups, industries, org authorities, governments, civic groups, partners of customers, and so on.

Example: Identifying Customers in a Disc Manufacturing Company.

Janrex Inc. manufactures optical discs for various applications. In the recent past, the organization received too many complaints from customers about the quality of its products. The majority of customers stated that they were not able organizations, and individual business owners who do not purchase or use the product but are impacted by it, such as regulatory to record data on some of the optical discs in a single pack. Therefore, the organization implemented Six Sigma in its entire process to improve the quality of the products. During the Six Sigma implementation, the Six Sigma team identified people involved in the electroforming process as internal customers because the electroforming process received inefficiently mastered optical discs from the glass mastering department. In glass mastering, information is encoded onto discs using laser beam recorders. In electroforming, the sensitive discs would be converted into hard and strong discs. Due to the inefficiently mastered optical discs received from the glass mastering department, the electroforming department was not able to manufacture high-quality optical discs.

Moreover, the Six Sigma team identified end users as the external customers of the process.

• • • • • •

Gather Customer Data

You will gather feedback from customers, even if your customers are unaware of the state-of-the-art developments in your organization, they can spark innovation in your products and services.

To gather your customer requirements accurately, you can apply different methods for gathering the Voice Of the Customer (VOC). Identifying customer expectations will help you determine the quality standards of your products or services.

What do you understand by Voice Of the Customer (VOC)?

The *voice of the customer (VOC)* is the process of capturing the stated and unstated needs or requirements of customers. By understanding the VOC, organizations can provide customers with products or services that are of superior value. Generally, customer voices are diverse and they must be considered, reconciled, and balanced to identify the quality attributes that need to be incorporated in a product or service. Unlike traditional approaches, the VOC emphasizes capturing the customer's voices verbatim, as far as possible. Sometimes the customers' body language may also convey valuable information. The VOC is a proactive way of capturing the customer's changing requirements with time. It is commonly captured through market research, interviews, questionnaires, and surveys. Other approaches to capturing the VOC include focus groups, mystery shopping, customer feedback and complaints data, reliability and warranty data, staff feedback, observations, and field reports.

Describe the various methods used for Gathering the VOC?

To gather the VOC, effective methods for accurately capturing customer requirements are required. Several methods are available to capture the VOC.

- **Interviews** are used to gather information from stakeholders by talking to them directly. Interviews aid in identifying and defining features and functions or desired project deliverables.
- **Focus groups** is a trained moderator-guided interactive discussion that includes pre-qualified stakeholders and subject-matter experts (SMEs) to elicit their expectations and attitudes toward the proposed product, service, or result of the project.

- **A facilitated workshop is** an interactive group-focused session that brings together key cross-functional stakeholders to define the project or product requirements. It is a primary technique to define cross-functional requirements and reconcile stakeholder differences to the project. Facilitated workshops occur much faster than individual discussions.
- *Questionnaires and surveys* is another method where written sets of questions designed to quickly gather information from a broad audience.
- *Mystery shopping* commonly performed in retail industries. This method is used to measure the quality of a service by gathering specific information about the product or service. This method is performed by mystery shoppers who introduce themselves as customers and perform specific customer-related tasks, such as purchasing a product and raising questions and complaints about the product.
- *Observations* are a direct way of viewing individuals in their work environment or while using the product to identify the project or product requirements. Also referred to as job shadowing.
- *Market research* is an organized effort to gather information about the current trends in an industry and also *Field reports* is a formal report documented by field engineers or other on-site personnel who gather required information about events that occur during their field work.
- *Customer feedback* and *complaints data* are used to gather customer requirements. This method also involves gathering customer feedback about the quality of a product or service. The consolidated list of feedback from customers is referred to as complaints data.
- *Reliability* data is a source of information that helps in analysing the reliability of a product or process. By gathering this data, you can plan strategies to gain a reputation with customers as a reliable provider of services.
- *Staff feedback* is another method of gathering opinions from staff who interacts with customers directly or who possess knowledge about customers and their expectations. This information is captured by conducting surveys, brainstorming sessions, and other information gathering sessions.

How to Gather Customer Data?

Well-defined goals are the best way to assure a good questionnaire design. When the goals of a study can be expressed in a few clear and concise sentences, the design of the questionnaire becomes considerably easier.

To effectively conduct a customer survey through a questionnaire, follow these guidelines:
- Keep your questionnaire short because long questionnaires get fewer responses when compared to short questionnaires.
- Include experts and relevant decision makers in the questionnaire design process.
- Formulate a plan for doing the statistical analysis during the design stage of the project.

- Questionnaires reflect first impressions. The respondent's first impressions come from the cover letter. Provide a well-written cover letter.
- Give your questionnaire a title that is short and meaningful to the respondents.
- Include clear and concise instructions on how to complete the questionnaire.
- Use short sentences and basic vocabulary.
- Begin with a few interesting items. If the first items are too boring, there is little chance that the questionnaire will be completed.
- Use simple and direct language in the questions so they are clearly understood by the respondents.
- Leave adequate space for respondents to make comments. One criticism of questionnaires is their inability to retain the connotation of responses.
- Place the most important items in the first half of the questionnaire.
- Hold the respondents' interest. One way to keep a questionnaire interesting is to use a variety of questions.
- Provide incentives as a motivation for a properly completed questionnaire.
- Make it convenient. The easier the questionnaire, the better the response.
- Use professional production methods for the questionnaire, such as desktop publishing.
- The final test of a questionnaire is to try it on representatives of the target audience to identify any problem areas.

Example: Gathering Customer Data.
Ristell & Rudison Inc. is a leading manufacturer of white boards. The company supplies a wide variety of white boards to the U.S. market. In order to understand customer's viewpoints and gather more data on customer requirements, the organization designed a questionnaire.

The questionnaire started with personal details such as name, occupation, communication details, and nationality. Then, questions on various topics were covered, including customer satisfaction levels for products and financial transactions, the aesthetic values of the products that customers use, customer resource management (CRM) aspects of the organization, the availability and delivery of products, a comparison of the quality of Ristell & Rudison products with those of other companies, recommendations and suggestions to improve products and services.

■ ■ ■ ■ ■

Analyze Customer Data
Now that you are familiar with gathering feedback from customers, you can proceed with analysing customer feedback using a variety of graphical, statistical, and qualitative tools. In this topic, you will analyze the VOC.

The implementation of Six Sigma in an organization is influenced by customer requirements. Successfully implementing Six Sigma not only requires you to be familiar with different methods of gathering the VOC, but also demands your ability to analyze the feedback provided by customers. Your familiarity with different graphical, statistical, and qualitative tools will help you accurately analyze customer data.

Broadly describe the tools for analysing Customer Data?

The main purpose of analysing customer data is to identify customer needs and requirements and prioritize the data based on the effective changes they will make in an entire process. You can use different kinds of tools to analyze customer data. The tools can be categorized into graphical, statistical, and qualitative tools.

Graphical Tool Type Design: These are software tools that help you visualize data patterns in graphical formats. Examples include bar charts, pie charts, and interrelationship diagrams.

Statistical Tool Type Design: These tools help you determine the summary and distribution values of a set of data. Some of the statistical tools include mean, median, average, mode, range, variance, and standard deviation.

Qualitative Tool Type Design: These tools help you identify the interrelationship among various categories of data. Examples include affinity diagrams; strengths, weaknesses, opportunities, and threats (SWOT) analysis; and prioritization matrices.

Analytical Tool Type	Description
Graphical tools	• Software tools that help visualize data patterns in graphical formats. • Examples include bar charts, pie charts, and interrelationship diagrams.
Statistical tools	• Help determine the summary and distribution values of a set of data. • Some tools include mean, median, average, mode, range, variance, and, standard deviation.
Qualitative tools	• Help identify the interrelationship among various categories of data. • Examples include affinity diagrams; strengths, weaknesses, opportunities, and threats (SWOT) analysis; and prioritization matrices.

What are Affinity Diagrams?

An *affinity diagram* is a tool that is used to organize a large number of ideas, opinions, and issues and group them based on their relationships. Affinity diagrams are generally used for categorizing ideas that are generated during brainstorming sessions and can be particularly useful for analysing complex issues.

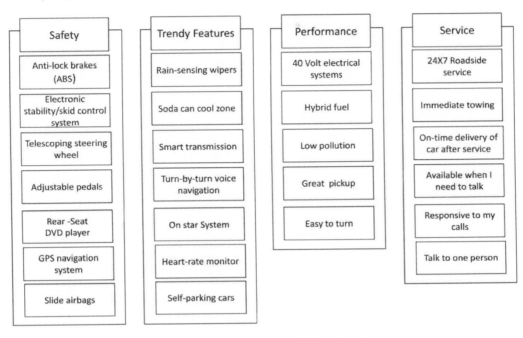

Fig: Example of Affinity Diagram

The steps for creating an affinity diagram can include:
1. Generating ideas through brainstorming.
2. Displaying the ideas randomly.
3. Sorting the ideas into groups.
4. Creating header cards for each group to capture the essential links among the ideas in each group.
5. And, drawing the affinity diagram by writing the problem statement at the top and the headers with their respective groups of ideas below the problem statement.
6. An affinity diagram helps in sorting and grouping customer requirements.

How to analyze customer data using the Affinity Diagram?

1. Generate ideas. Use brainstorming to generate a list of ideas. The rest of the steps in the affinity process will be easier if these ideas are written on sticky notes.
2. Display the ideas. Post the ideas on a wall randomly.
3. Sort the ideas into related groups using the following process:
   a. Start by looking for two ideas that seem related in some way. Place them together in a column on one side.

51

b. Look for ideas that are related to those you have already set aside and add them to that group.
c. Look for other ideas that are related to each other and establish new groups.
d. Repeat the previous steps until your team has placed all of the ideas in groups.
4. Create headers for the groups. A header is an idea that captures the essential link among the ideas contained in a group of sticky notes.
5. Draw the finished affinity diagram.
6. Document the finished affinity diagram.

· · · · ·

Translate Customer Requirements

In the previous topic, you analysed customer data. Now, you want to translate the expectations of customers in terms of quality characteristics and attributes. In this topic, you will translate the requirements of customers. To improve the quality of a product or service, it is essential to gather feedback from customers and identify characteristics that satisfy your customers' requirements.

Familiarity with several characteristics that are critical to the quality of a product or service will ensure the successful execution of your Six Sigma project. Many times QFD, is also considered as a tool for translating customer requirements.

Requirements Statements

Requirements statements are concise statements that include the details of customer requirements. These statements enable the team to identify underlying issues, metrics, and standards in the process. Requirements statements can be easily read and understood by anyone involved in the Six Sigma project because they do not include complex technical jargon and keywords that are included in statements that are part of the VOC gathering process.

Creating effective requirements statements is a very critical step because you have to articulate the customer's voice, and if you interpret or translate it incorrectly, the entire product or service could be designed or redesigned incorrectly.

CTQ Attributes

Some of the major attributes of CTQ include:
- A single meaning for each metric across all geographic locations.
- Defining the process owners who are responsible for tracking the CTQ.
- Clearly defined defects and opportunities in the process.
- A consistent measurement system to provide accurate and precise measurements.
- And, it must be derived from the VOC so that it provides a strong linkage to the VOC.

How to Translate Customer Requirements?

From the VOC received, the project team or the process owner has to extract key customer requirements or underlying issues or concerns that customers have with a product or service.

To translate customer requirements, follow these guidelines:
- Avoid statements in a negative form.
- Avoid two-valued concepts such as yes/no types.
- Avoid abstract words such as "reliable" or "durable."
- Avoid statements which have solutions in them.
- Avoid premature details such as "end of day is 5.30 p.m."
- Avoid the auxiliary verbs such as "should" or "must."
- Avoid intangible concepts.

. . . . .

Identify Six Sigma Projects

In the previous topic, you translated customer requirements into quality characteristics and attributes. Based on the CTQs, you want to identify projects that require the implementation of Six Sigma.

In this topic, you will identify Six Sigma projects. Not all projects in your organization will require the implementation of Six Sigma. As a Six Sigma professional, your work involves identifying and prioritizing projects in your organization that require the implementation of Six Sigma. Analysing project types and their priority for the organization will help you make this decision.

Describe the Project Selection Process

Selecting the right Six Sigma project can help your business in various ways, including significant business process improvements and a large *return on investment (ROI)*. The Six Sigma project selection process involves:

1. Identifying opportunities for improvement in a range of organizational areas such as production, operations, finance, and strategy.
2. Analysing opportunities and grouping related opportunities together.
3. Evaluating and ranking opportunities for improvement against two criteria: resources needed to implement projects and potential benefits in terms of ROI after completing the projects.
4. And, choosing those projects that rank higher for implementing Six Sigma.

What are the common methods for selecting projects?

Six Sigma projects are selected on the basis of their impact on the organization's bottom line. Only a few project selection methods are available.

- **Criteria-based method** uses a weighted selection matrix used rate projects on criteria decided by stakeholders and customers.
- **Pareto diagram** is a prioritization tool also known as the 80-20 rule is used in this method.
- **Hoshin Kanri** is a method used for deploying organizational strategies and identifying projects that will help an organization achieve its goals.

What the sources of improvement projects?

Six Sigma projects are primarily focused on customers. The other areas that Six Sigma projects focus on are:

- Improving the performance of *Critical to Quality (CTQ)* characteristics.
- Reducing the number of complaints from customers.
- Reducing in-process or internal defects.
- Reducing warranty claims.
- Improving survey and customer research scores.
- Capturing feedback from staff members effectively.
- Increasing profits and revenue.
- Improving audit scores.
- Improving process performance and dashboard metrics.
- And, having better growth than competitors.

What the key criteria for project selection?

The criteria for selecting projects are primarily based on customer needs and the organization's business strategies. Other criteria include:

- Project duration. Usually, projects that are less than four months in duration are preferred when selecting projects.
- A focus on core businesses.
- And, a well-defined and manageable project scope.

Describe the Project Selection Process

Selecting the right project can help your business in various ways, including significant business process improvement and large ROIs.

The Six Sigma project selection process involves:

- Identifying opportunities for improvement in a range of areas such as operations, finance, and organizational strategy.
- Analysing opportunities and grouping related opportunities together.

- Evaluating and ranking opportunities for improvement against two criteria: the resources needed to implement the projects and the potential benefits in terms of ROI after completing the projects.
- And, choosing those projects that rank higher for implementing Six Sigma.

Explain Pareto Charts

A *Pareto chart* is a bar chart or histogram that is used to rank causes of problems in a hierarchical format. The goal is to narrow down the primary causes of variation and focus the efforts of a Six Sigma project on tackling the most significant sources of variation. The variables in the Pareto chart are ordered by frequency of occurrence. Besides the main bar graph, the Pareto chart also includes a line graph that represents the cumulative percentage of occurrences at each bar. This line graph is used to determine which of the bars are vital few and which ones are trivial many. Pareto charts can be very useful tools for prioritizing and focusing corrective actions throughout the entire project.

Example: A Pareto Chart Representing Causes of Failures.
A typical Pareto chart is used to represent data, which is first organized in descending order of occurrence and then plotted along a cumulative curve. The bars represent the number of failures for each of the causes (A through E). In this example, approximately 72 percent of the total number of failures is due to causes A and B (320 out of 440). The project team can easily see that they should focus most of their corrective action efforts on those two causes.

Share guidelines identify six sigma projects?

The success of Six Sigma implementation hinges upon selecting the right projects in your business processes. Though different organizations have different criteria for selecting projects, there are a few common practices that organizations generally follow.

Fig: Pareto Chart

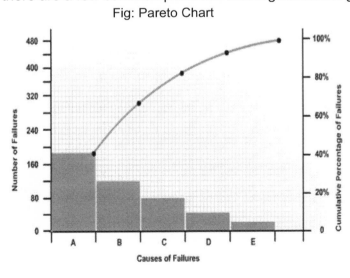

Causes of Failures

To select Six Sigma projects, follow these guidelines:
- Select projects in trouble areas where a considerable amount of time is spent on solving recurring problems. These trouble areas offer excellent opportunities for improving processes.
- Ensure that the projects are related to the strategic goals of your organization.
- The result of the project should be linked to improving core business strategies or processes.

- Verify if the defects can be identified and measured. This is necessary to validate the reduction in the number of defects.
- Make sure that the entire process is clearly defined with specific start and end points.
- Check if business metrics, such as on-time delivery, cycle time goals, and cost reduction goals, are clearly defined.
- The projects that you choose should also be reasonable in size. Pick projects that are large enough for process improvements but small enough to manage.
- Analyze whether the project can be completed within a reasonable period.
- Ideally, Six Sigma projects should be completed within six months. However, if the scope of the project is global in nature, the completion can take up to eight months.
- Determine if statistical tools can be applied to the project so that the performance can be measured and quantified. By analysing the data collected, you can gain a better understanding of the variables involved.
- Ensure that the project has the support of the champion. As a key member of the Six Sigma team, his or her support is important for the success of Six Sigma projects.
- Identify a process owner who will be responsible for the entire process and has the authority to determine how it must function.
- Before selecting a project, verify if internal and external customers can be identified.
- Identifying customers is imperative to the organization because it helps determine if their requirements are met.

Example: Selection of Six Sigma Projects in a Memory Chip Manufacturing Company.
Janrex Inc., a leading memory chip manufacturing company for nearly a decade, has been facing a decline in its annual sales for the past two years. Faced with stiff competition in the industry, the company was under considerable pressure to maintain its position as a market leader. After considering various quality improvement programs, such as Total Quality Management (TQM) and quality circle, the organization decided to implement Six Sigma to achieve its goal. The organization formed a Six Sigma team and gave it the responsibility of selecting appropriate projects where Six Sigma could be successfully deployed.

The Six Sigma team began the project selection process by analysing all relevant data to identify the problem areas in the entire process. The team identified that the sales department received an increasing number of complaints from customers regarding defective products in the market. The team set a goal of cutting down the defects to the Six Sigma level of 3.4 defects per million opportunities and identified projects where the Six Sigma methodology could be implemented to meet this objective. The team also ensured that specific statistical tools, such as flowcharts and run charts, could be applied to measure and control the performance of projects.

■ ■ ■ ■ ■

4 Six Sigma Project Charter

Identifying a Six Sigma project involves charting the key elements that will measure the success of a Six Sigma project. A project charter can provide a clear roadmap for the successful completion of a project. In this topic, you will draft a project charter. A project charter provides a clear framework for the project-specific and business goals of a Six Sigma project. In order to execute the Six Sigma project successfully, you need to apply the fundamentals of drafting a project charter.

Six Sigma Project

A *project* is a temporary work endeavour that creates a unique product, service, or result. It has a clearly defined beginning and an end. The end of a project is reached when its objectives are met, the need for the project no longer exists, or it is determined that the objectives cannot be met. Projects can vary widely in terms of budget, team size, duration, expected outcomes, and industries.

Example: The FPY Improvement Project.

Rudison Inc., a leading tape drive manufacturer, has been facing a decline in its annual sales for the past two years. With stiff competition in the industry, the company was under considerable pressure to maintain its position as a market leader. As a consequence, the company wanted to implement the Six Sigma methodology to improve processes. Based on the initial analysis, the Six Sigma team defined the first pass yield (FPY) improvement process as the Six Sigma project. The project's goal was to improve FPY from 56 percent to 94 percent within the next four months.

Characteristics of a Project

Every project has certain characteristics that differentiate it from other projects. A few characteristics are listed below.

- Projects are undertaken to create a lasting outcome.
- Projects have clearly defined beginning and end points.
- Projects have a finite time frame to produce the expected outcome.
- Projects have resources allocated according to need. The team is disbanded when the project ends with unique products, services, or results.
- Project deliveries produce products or artefacts that become the end item or a component item.
- Deliver services to business functions supports production or distribution.
- Projects produce results as outcomes or documents.

Define Project Charter

A *project charter* is a contract between a Six Sigma project team and a sponsor. It provides a clear, concise description of the business needs that the project is intended to address. Any changes to the critical elements of a project charter need prior approval from the sponsor and consensus from the team members.

What are elements of a Project Charter?

A Six Sigma project charter includes different elements such as the business case, problem statement, scope of the project, goal statement, potential benefits, tollgates, and team members.

- **Business case:** A description that provides a background of the process and product or service. The objective of the business case is to highlight the current situation and provide a justification to change the current state. The business case further highlights the urgency to change the current state.
- **Problem statement:** A description of the problem or opportunity that the project must address. It underlines the reasons for implementing the project in your organization.
- **Project scope:** A description of the scope of work that the project must include. It can also specify what the project will and will not include.
- **Goal statement:** A description of the objectives of the project. The goals of a project should be SMART: Specific, Measurable, Achievable, Realistic, and Time-bound.
- **Potential benefits:** The key benefits that would be obtained by implementing the project. They help garner the support of management to allocate necessary resources to implement the project.
- **Tollgates:** Milestones for tasks that need to be completed at each phase of the DMAIC methodology. They help in planning a project properly and completing it on time.
- **Team members:** All the people who will be part of the project team. The roles of Six Sigma team members include an approver, a resource, a member, and an interested party.

How to Draft a Project Charter?

An effective project charter clearly communicates a Six Sigma project's importance to the organization and formally authorizes the project. To create an effective project charter, follow these guidelines:

- Use a corporate template, if one exists at your company.
- Build a business case that shows the importance of the project in relation to the goals of your organization.
- Define the problem statement. Include a brief description of the opportunity or problem area that the project is intended to address.
- Include a goal statement that describes the expected results of the project.
- Include a project scope that clearly states the boundaries of the project.

Project Name	Installation TAT reduction			Project Number	
Process Name	Service Delivery	**Green Belt**			
Sub Process Name	Installation	**Sponsor**			

Business Case	Problem / Opportunity Statement	Goal Statement
For Clearcalls, over the past 3 months the revenues started to drop by 20 -25% compared to the previous year. There are other associated issues such as employee attrition, increasing trend of complaints, drop in service levels. Further JustmakeCalls, and AnytimeNet are setting up their broadband service lines and will be opening over the next two months. As a result it is critical to address the root cause for dropping revenues and arrest them immediately.	Based on the Voice of Customers, it's clear that the Turnaround Time (TAT) from request to installation of broadline is very high and customers are unhappy. Current TAT is very high and beyond 30 hours. This problem seems to be prevalent for over 6 months now.	Reduce the TAT for request to installation from XX hours to less than 24 hours within the next 3 months.

Project Scope Includes	Project Excludes	Project Milestones				
- All regions - Walk-in and online sales - Submission of application to installation completion	- Remote location installations - Customer door lock cases	**Start Date:**			**End Date:**	
			Target Date	Actual Date	Toll gate Review Date	
		Define	1/5			
		Measure	2/5			
		Analyze	2/25			
		Improve	3/15			
		Control	4/10			

Project CTQ Details					Project Comments	
					Nil	

Primary CTQs		Unit	Target	
Installation TAT		Hours	30 hours	

Secondary CTQs				Project Charter Sign Off (With date)
Installation complaints		%	2%	Sponsor
				GB/BB
				BB/QL

Project Translation Plans	Project Benefits Estimate
Replication to landline processes	Increased revenue and reduced complaints from customers. Improved Customer Satisfaction Scores

Fig: Project Charter

- Explain what the project will and will not include.
- Include summary descriptions of the potential benefits that the project would bring to the product or service.
- Provide a list of project tollgates.
- List milestones for each phase of the DMAIC methodology.
- Include the team members who will be a part of the Six Sigma project and their roles.

- List the team members under the roles of approver, resource, member, and interested party.
- Include the amount of time that each team member would spend on the project.
- Ensure that the person who has the required knowledge and authority signs the project charter.
- Distribute the signed charter to appropriate project stakeholders, including: Project team members, Customers and, if relevant, sellers (vendors), Relevant functional managers, Finance department, accounting department, or both.

Example: Creating a Six Sigma Project Charter. (Ref to Fig- Project Charter)
Having identified problems in the packaging process, the management of a food processing company decided to implement a Six Sigma project to rectify the problems. Management asked the Six Sigma team to create a charter that will formally authorize the project and establish its priority. The name of the project in the charter and the charter's date serves as the authorization date. The charter describes the need for implementing the Six Sigma project. It includes the problem statement, objectives, scope, and benefits of the project. The team members and their roles are also included in the charter. Once the charter is signed, it is distributed to all the stakeholders and project managers involved in the project.

. . . . . .

Project Scope

In the previous topic, you drafted a project charter. At this stage, you will determine the project scope at a preliminary level; it helps prevent the Six Sigma project from veering off its baseline and improvement goals. In this topic, you will develop the project scope.

The project scope determines major deliverables, assumptions, objectives, and project constraints that form the basis of decisions regarding the execution of the Six Sigma project. By developing the scope of a project, you can easily determine the timeline and cost of the Six Sigma project and reduce misunderstandings regarding the goals of the project.

The project scope is a set of agreed-upon project characteristics and boundaries that define the project and what it does and does not need to accomplish. The best way to scope a project is by having an open-minded conversation with all stakeholders and involved parties of the project. Scoping ensures that the project team is concentrating on the best opportunity for process improvement. It is normally done by Black Belts or Green Belts with assistance from a Master Black Belt or Sponsor. In Six Sigma, Pareto charts and the In Frame/Out Frame diagram are the most common tools used to scope a project.

Example: The Scope of a Six Sigma Project in Manufacturing.
Ristell Corp., a leading garment manufacturer in the U.S., has been manufacturing printed T-shirts since 1970. In the recent past, the company faced a decline in profits and management

was forced to take a second look at the existing process to improve revenue. In order to improve the process, management implemented a Six Sigma project. During implementation, the Six Sigma project team evaluated the VOC and drafted a project charter. The VOC stated that on-time shipping and image centering were the major CTQs (Critical To Quality) of the project. Based on the CTQs, the team defined the project scope, which included reducing customer complaints and providing on-time shipping.

What the characteristics of project scope statements?

A project scope statement is a statement that describes a project and what it does and does not need to accomplish. The project scope statement is created at an early stage of the project to reflect the stakeholders' common understanding of major activities to be performed in the project, and to provide a basis for future project decisions about what should and should not be included in the project. Depending upon the size and scope of the project, a project scope statement should typically include:

- Project objectives, deliverables, and requirements.
- Project constraints and assumptions.
- And, product acceptance criteria.

Example: The Project Scope Statement of a Six Sigma Project.

As part of Six Sigma implementation at Ristell Corp., the project team drafted the project scope statement as follows:

- Reduce customer complaints based on the price and period.
- Reduce on-time shipping time.

This clearly conveys the boundaries and limitations of this project. The project team excluded fabric quality from the scope statement because customers select the fabric quality in the market.

Describe In Frame/Out Frame Diagram

The *In Frame/Out Frame diagram* is a project management tool that is used to define the scope of a Six Sigma project. The tool considers three aspects: in the frame, on the frame, and out of the frame.

In the frame aspects are variables in a process that are included as part of the scope of the project. On the frame aspects are undecided variables in the process that can be treated as a parking lot for future debates during brainstorming sessions. Out of the frame aspects are variables in the process that can be excluded from the scope of the project.

How to Develop the Project Scope using In Frame/Out Frame diagram?

1. Draw a large square picture frame on a flip chart.
2. List activities pertaining to the process on sticky notes with one sticky for each activity.

3. Sort out the sticky notes based on whether they fall within the scope or outside the scope.
4. Some aspects about the scope may not be clear up front. Place these aspects on the frame for the time being.
5. With the team, discuss whether the on the frame aspects can be pulled into the frame or pushed out of the frame.
6. If necessary, debate with team members about what should be included or not included within the scope. Some topics for inclusion could be resources, timing, organizations involved, team members, process impacted, target results, and so on.

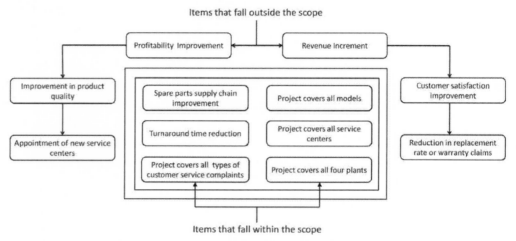

Fig: Example of In Frame-Out Frame diagram

■ ■ ■ ■ ■

Identify Project Metrics

In the previous topic, you developed the project scope. It is important to measure project deliverables in order to e evaluate the performance of the Six Sigma project. In this topic, you will identify key project metrics. How will you measure the performance improvements of a Six Sigma project? You need a set of key project metrics that you can use to measure the project's performance at various stages. By identifying such metrics, you can capture the potential components of project value and complete the project efficiently.

What the project metrics and how are they useful?

A *project metric* is the measurement of a particular characteristic of the performance or efficiency of a project. The metrics of a Six Sigma project reflect customer needs and ensure that the internal metrics of the organization are achieved. The selection of project metrics is one of the crucial elements in the Define phase of the Six Sigma methodology.

Project metrics should be simple, meaningful, straightforward, and understood by all members of the Six Sigma team. The Six Sigma team understands the problem statement, identifies various metrics, and finally decides the metrics that help them achieve better results. Six Sigma project metrics can be categorized into primary metrics and secondary metrics.

Example: Project Metrics of a Six Sigma Project.
Janrex Inc., a leading chip manufacturing company, was facing a decline in its annual sales for the past two years. Faced with stiff competition in the industry, the company was under considerable pressure to maintain its position as a market leader. As a consequence, the company wanted to implement the Six Sigma methodology to improve the process. During the Define phase, the project team identified the Six Sigma project and its metrics. Some of the project metrics include customer satisfaction, cost of poor quality, and cycle time.

What do you understand by Primary Metrics?

A *primary metric,* also called a project CTQ, is a CTQ measure that is used to monitor project progression and success. It is the reference point throughout the Six Sigma project. Ideally, project CTQs should have direct impact on customers. For any Six Sigma project, the primary metrics should be:

- Tied to the problem statement and objective of the project.
- In possession of an operational definition.
- Measurable, simple, and expressed in the form of an equation.
- Aligned to business objectives.
- Tracked on hourly, daily, weekly, and monthly basis.
- Expressed graphically over time with a run chart, time series, or control chart.
- And, validated with a Measurement Systems Analysis (MSA).

Some of the primary metrics of a Six Sigma project include customer satisfaction, on-time delivery of products, final product quality, and less costly products.

What do you understand by Secondary Metrics?

A *secondary metric,* also known as a consequential metric, is a project metric that you do not want to sacrifice at the expense of primary improvements in a process. These metrics ensure that the process is improving and not shifting one metric at the expense of another. It means that the secondary metrics have a relationship with the primary metrics of a Six Sigma project. Therefore, the primary goal of a Six Sigma project will be to move the primary metrics, but ensure that secondary metrics do not deteriorate or stay constant. Some of the secondary metrics include cycle time, volume shipped, inspection data, and rework hours. These metrics should not be sacrificed to achieve the primary metrics such as customer satisfaction, on-time delivery of products, and final product quality.

■ ■ ■ ■ ■

Identify Project Planning Tools

In the previous topic, you identified project metrics that measure performance improvements. Now, it is time to identify project planning tools that ensure the successful completion of a Six Sigma project. In this topic, you will identify project planning tools. Without knowing what to do in your job, it is hard for you to reach your destination. To achieve your goal, you need to define the course of action that you propose to undertake during any of your activities. A well-thought-out plan will give you an idea about what is to be done, how it is to be done, and when it is to be done. Similarly, the successful execution of a Six Sigma project depends on effective planning, which in turn depends on using the right project planning tools.

Describe the role of project schedules in Six Sigma projects?

A *project schedule* is the project team's plan for starting and finishing activities on specific dates and in a certain sequence. The schedule also specifies planned dates for meeting project milestones. The purpose of the project schedule is to coordinate activities to form a master plan in order to complete project objectives on time. It is also used to track the performance schedule and keep upper management and project stakeholders informed about the project's status

Task	Activity	Duration in days
0	Six Sigma Project	Objective
0,1	Gather customer feedback	7
0,3	Identify resources & on-board	15
1,3	Define process objectives & scope	7
3,4	Process mapping	7
3,5	Identify quick hits	6
5,10	Implement quick hit solutions	50
4,6	Collect data	30
7,8	Generate solutions	4
8,9	Shortlist and pilot solutions	15
9,10	Gather pilot feedback from market	4
8,10	Risk mitigation	10
10,11	Launch of new solutions	45
11,13	Monitor Results	30
11,12	Update process documentation	7
12,13	Train & institutionalize new process	1
13	Project closure	Milestone

Example: Schedule Performance

Consider a software development project. The estimated duration of the entire project is four months. The project manager, Dan, decides that there will be eight reporting periods early in the project life cycle and that work package owners will supply schedule performance reports every two weeks.

What are Gantt Charts?

A *Gantt chart* is a project planning and scheduling tool that provides up-to-date summary information of a Six Sigma project. It can be extremely helpful for analysing the project's overall time performance. The Gantt chart also shows when milestones are scheduled and if those critical dates are still on track. The project is broken down into smaller tasks with their respective labels. The approximate time required to complete each task is derived by using a formula.

The formula is: [The optimistic time needed + (4 x The expected time needed) + The pessimistic time needed] / 6.

Gantt charts are modified throughout the process to know the actual progress of the project.

Describe Critical Path Method (CPM)

The *Critical Path Method (CPM)* is a project planning and scheduling tool that demonstrates the chronological tasks of a Six Sigma project and helps estimate the predetermined time to start and finish key project tasks. The path with the longest duration and no scheduling flexibility is the critical path. Activities on the critical path cannot be delayed or the whole project will be delayed unless subsequent activities are shortened. A single project can have multiple critical paths.

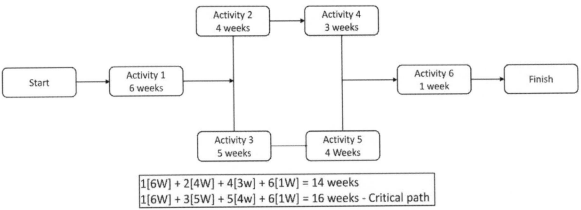

Fig: Critical path method

Describe PERT Method

The *Program Evaluation and Review Technique (PERT)* is a project management technique that is used to analyze the tasks involved and identify the minimum time required to complete each activity in a Six Sigma project. The technique involves breaking down the project into activities, identifying their relationships, sequencing the activities, and defining their duration. Information collected using PERT is represented in the form of a network diagram. It contains project milestones and paths that connect these milestones. PERT is generally used for project scheduling and does not help find the shortest way to complete a project. The PERT chart uses a weighted average of the three estimate types (most likely, optimistic, and pessimistic) to calculate the expected activity duration. PERT considers five parameters to schedule each task of a Six Sigma project.

Parameter	Description
ES	• Denotes Early Start. The earliest time an activity can start. • Usually, the ES of the first activity is zero.
EF	• Denotes Early Finish. • The earliest time an activity can finish.
LF	• Denotes Late Finish. The latest time an activity can finish. • The LF for the last activity is the same as its EF time.
LS	• Denotes Late Start. The latest time an activity can start. • The LS for the last activity is its EF minus its duration.
DU	• Denotes Duration. • The number of work periods required for the completion of an activity

What is meant by the term Float in project management?

Float, also called slack, is the amount of time an activity can be delayed from its ES without delaying the project finish date or the consecutive activities. Float occurs only in activities that are not on the critical path. There are two types of float: total and free. Total float is the total amount of time an activity can be delayed without delaying the project finish date. Total float for an activity can be calculated by subtracting its EF from its LF or its ES from its LS. Free float is the amount of time an activity can be delayed without delaying the ES of any activity that immediately follows it. Free float for an activity is calculated by subtracting the EF of the activity from the ES of its successor activity.

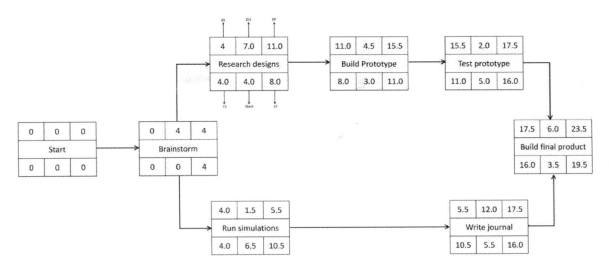

Fig: Float in project management

What is the difference between CPM & PERT?

CPM uses a sequential start-to-finish network logic, while PERT identifies the minimum time required to complete each activity in a Six Sigma project.

Six Sigma Project Tollgate Reviews

A *tollgate review* is a checkpoint in a Six Sigma project that determines whether work for a particular phase of the DMAIC methodology has been performed as described in the project plan and indicates the readiness of the project's entry into the next phase. It also checks whether the goals within each phase have been achieved successfully and adhere to the organization's strategic goals.

The tollgate review is performed after each stage of the DMAIC methodology to ensure that the project is successful. The tollgate review is performed by a Master Black Belt with Green Belts, Black Belts, the Champion or Sponsor, and other appropriate team members. During tollgate reviews, the Six Sigma team tracks and realizes the benefits obtained in each phase, reviews the program risks and issues, and provides constructive measures. Some of the tools that are used to perform a tollgate review include Check sheets, Milestone charts, and, project deliverable charts, such as Gantt and PERT charts, and the project schedule.

Describe Project Management Plans

A *project management plan* is a plan that details how a project will be executed to achieve its objectives. A well-defined plan consists of certain components, including:

- A list of the project management processes that will be utilized and the level of implementation for each.
- A description of the tools and techniques that will be used to complete those processes.

WBS	Tasks	Owner	Plan Start	Plan Finish	Days	FTEs	Hrs.	Month-1					Month-2			
								5-3	5-10	5-17	5-24	5-31	6-7	6-14	6-21	6-28
1	**Project Name**						489									
1.1	**Project planning & prep**		**04-May-10**	**01-Aug-10**												
1.1.1	Supervison & coord	AA	5/3/20010	01-Aug-10	0	0.40	0									
1.1.2	Develop plan	AA	04-May-10	28-May-10	0	0.30	0									
1.1.3	Develop budget	BB	24-May-10	03-Jun-10	0	0.20	0									
1.1.4	Schedule kickoff mtg.	DD	17-May-10	17-May-10	0	0.20	0									
1.1.5	Conduct kickoff mtg.	CC	07-Jun-10	07-Jun-10	0	8.00	0									
1.1.6	Monthly Meetings	CC			6	4.00	192									
1.1.7	Quarterly Mtgs.	CC			2	4.00	64									
1.2	**Requirements Management**															
1.2.1	**Conduct requirements analysis**		**24-May-10**	**13-Jul-10**												
	Develop interview forms	BB	24-May-10	28-May-10	0	2.00	0									
	Conduct interviews	CC	28-May-10	25-Jun-10	0	4.00	0									
	Write prelim. requirements	NN	14-Jun-10	02-Jul-10	0	1.00	0									
	Conduct walk-thru	CC	06-Jul-10	07-Jul-10	0	8.00	0									
	Update requirements doc.	NN	08-Jul-10	13-Jul-10	0	2.00	0									

Fig: Project management plan

- An extensive description of the tasks to be completed to fulfil the objectives.
- Plans for monitoring and controlling changes to the project.
- Performance measurement baselines.
- Techniques for communication with stakeholders.
- A definition of the project life cycle.
- And, a plan for identifying, documenting, and addressing open issues.

Project management plans may be a detailed or simple summary and may include any number of subsidiary management plans.

Example: The Project Management Plan for a Six Sigma Project
A manufacturer of piston pins sought to reduce customer complaints and defects. The steering council decided that this project would be run as a Green Belt project. The Green Belt who led this project is the project manager, and he was mentored by a Black Belt. The Green Belt put out a detailed project management plan.

The project management plan consisted of the DMAIC tollgates, activities thought to be necessary, and the Six Sigma tools to be used to complete the DMAIC phases. The plan also listed the tasks to be completed including data collection, root cause analysis, solutions generation, implementation, and plans for controlling project changes. A project charter was created to establish the business case, problem statement, goal statement, scope, approvers, team members, and timelines for different phases. The Steering Council was the final approving authority of the project and they reviewed the project at the end of every phase through a formal tollgate. On approval, the project progressed to the next phase of the project.

A *milestone chart* is a chart that provides a summary-level view of a project's schedule in terms of its milestones. It uses an icon or symbol to show scheduled milestone events. Milestones are typically listed from the left to right of the chart.

Time intervals—divided into hours, days, weeks, or months—are usually presented horizontally across the top or bottom of the chart. Milestone charts are effective at demonstrating the project's overall schedule to project team members, stakeholders, and upper management.

■ ■ ■ ■ ■

Project Documentation

In the previous topic, you identified project planning tools. Now, you want to explore how a project is completely documented. In this topic, you will describe project documentation. For any project, numerous document types are used and range from planning and tracking to reporting. How you manage these project documents determines the success or failure of a Six Sigma project. By compiling project documents, you can facilitate discussions on important issues in the project; record agreements on certain principles, actions, and changes within the project; and communicate the project status and issues to stakeholders of the project.

Role of Project Documentation

Documentation of a Six Sigma project is maintained throughout its implementation. The initial project document is the project proposal, which includes the objectives, project plan, and budget. During the implementation of a Six Sigma project, the project charter and status reports are generated, which serve as the communication vehicle to management on the progress and health of the project.

In addition, project documents help the Six Sigma team understand the main requirements for implementing the project on time. In addition, documents enable management to analyze the performance of the project and to decide the actions to be taken to achieve the desired results. All these documents are stored in a central repository during project implementation and will be archived as soon as the project is completed.

Some of the important information that is documented during the Six Sigma implementation includes:
- The project charter.
- The Statement of Work (SOW).
- Plans and schedules for projects and subprojects.
- Correspondence.
- Written agreements.
- Meeting minutes.

- Action items and responsibilities.
- Budgets and financial reports.
- Cost-benefit analyses.
- Status reports.
- Changes made to plans and budgets.
- Procedures followed or developed.
- And, notes of significant lessons learned.

Project Documentation Tools

Tools or methods for planning, monitoring, analysing, and controlling projects range from manual techniques to automated methods.

Manual techniques include using plain paper, graph paper, storyboards, white boards, colored magnetic markers, and so on.

Automated methods include using Microsoft® Excel®, Microsoft® Project®, and other specific project management software. Software packages accept dates, duration, costs, and available resources; determine resource conflicts and project estimated costs; and present data in a variety of formats including tables, Gantt charts, and network diagrams.

· · · · ·

Describe Project Risk Analysis

In the previous topic, you identified project planning tools. Now, you want to identify risks involved in the execution of a project. Moreover, you want to perform a systematic risk analysis to identify, manage, and mitigate risks in the project. In this topic, you will describe project risk analysis.

In any project, risks exist as a result of uncertainties. Risks can be identified by performing a project risk analysis. If undertaken correctly, the project risk analysis will help you identify various risks in a Six Sigma project and enable you to complete it successfully.

What is Project Risk Analysis?

Project risk analysis is the evaluation of the probability and impact of risk occurrence in a Six Sigma project. Risk analysis is typically conducted through either qualitative or quantitative techniques. The level of risk to the project is the product of the probability of the risk occurring and the predicted impact that the risk will have on the project's success.

Example: Project Risk Analysis for a Six Sigma Project

An automobile manufacturing company conducts various kinds of risk analysis before implementing Six Sigma. It evaluates the probability and impact of the risks that are associated with the Six Sigma project, which may include the costs of implementation, the potential revenue after the implementation, fluctuating consumer demands, and competition from rivals.

What is the purpose of Project Risk Analysis?

The main purpose of project risk analysis is to increase the likelihood of successful completion of a project in terms of cost, time, and performance objectives. Qualitative analysis enables the identification of main sources or factors of risks in the project.

Meanwhile, quantitative analysis brings out benefits in terms of understanding the project and its problems irrespective of whether or not a quantitative analysis is carried out. Some of the benefits of project risk analysis are:

- Lowering cost and confusion. By assessing risks in advance, you can reduce the cost impact due to the failure. Further, you can reduce a lot of confusion in the project by formulating realistic plans in terms of cost estimates and time scales.
- Prioritization and stakeholder support. By quantifying risks, you can prioritize and garner support from stakeholders for high risks.
- Risk mitigation. You can assess contingencies that reflect risks and hedge the risks.
- Setting expectations and establishing reserves. You can plan for high failure rates and increase buffers.
- And, communication and control. Appropriate communication will enable you to establish sufficient control over projects.

• • • • •

Project Closure

In the previous topic, you described project risk analysis. Now, you want to identify the project completion criteria. Typically, by describing a project closure, you can identify project completion criteria. This, in turn, helps identify performance improvements and additional opportunities. In this topic, you will describe project closure. Project closure is a formal project summation in which the project team can officially close the project. It allows for the quick handover of deliverables and documentation. Inefficiently done, it will reduce the level of project success and incorrectly identify additional opportunities.

What the steps involved in project closure process?

The *project closure* process involves closing out all project activities after the Control phase of a Six Sigma project and it consists of five steps:

1. The process starts with gathering the project team, which consists of all Belts involved in the project. The team updates the relevant records and reports of the various phases of the Six Sigma project. The project team also establishes procedures that help validate and document deliverables and formalize acceptance of those deliverables.

2. The Master Black Belt reviews all documents and the project management plan to ensure that all project work is complete, the objectives are met, and the deliverables are achieved.
3. The process owner verifies project results by comparing them with customer and stakeholder expectations and requirements and conducts financial audits. The process owner also tracks down the results of the project including process metrics and financial savings.
4. Using the project results and the inputs from team members, the Green Belt prepares best practices and lessons learned reports and writes a final report or presentation of the project.
5. The process owner officially declares the closure of the project.

Describe the role of closeout meetings in six sigma projects?

Closeout meetings are sessions held during the project closeout process and they involve all the stakeholders of the project. During a closeout meeting, the participants discuss the work and capture lessons learned and the best practices of the Six Sigma implementation. Based on the outcome of the meetings, the process owner will prepare a Six Sigma case study of the project. Closeout meetings typically follow a formal agenda and may require official minutes to be recorded. Not all organizations or projects require closeout meetings. Some organizations require the minutes from closeout meetings to be completed in full, approved by management, and preserved in a specific manner.

How are lessons learned report prepared?

Lessons learned reports are documents that capture salient and helpful information about work done in a project or project phase; they identify both the project team's strengths and areas for improvement. They can be formal or informal, depending on the organizational norms or requirements. They are compiled for the benefit of future project teams, so that people can capitalize on the organization's knowledge base about work that has already been done, avoid repeating mistakes, and benefit from ongoing organizational learning. Analyses include adequacy of personnel, time, equipment and money, effectiveness of the entire project, how well the project was tracked, how well top management and project sponsors were informed of the project's status, and how well the project team performed together.

• • • • • •

5 Interrelationship Digraph

You have gained knowledge about the fundamentals of project management. An interrelationship digraph is one of the tools used in a Six Sigma project for identifying relationships among different factors in a given group of data. In this topic, you will create an interrelationship digraph to determine how different factors in a given group of data are related to each other.

Once you categorize data relevant to different processes in your organization using an affinity diagram, you need to identify relationships among the different aspects in a category. By creating an interrelationship digraph that depicts the cause-and-effect relationship, you will be able to identify how different factors are connected to each other in a particular group of data when complex issues arise.

Understanding Interrelationship Digraphs

An *interrelationship digraph,* also called a *relations diagram* or *network diagram*, is a tool that depicts relationships among different elements, areas, or processes through a network of boxes and arrows. It is usually used by Six Sigma teams to understand cause-and-effect relationships among different factors of a problem.

Different factors associated with a problem are entered in boxes or written on sticky notes. Factors related to one another are placed close to each other. If any factor causes or influences any other factors, then an arrow is drawn from that factor to those affected factors. At the end of the exercise, the arrows are counted. Generally, boxes with the most arrows leading to them are the major issues. However, this is not a hard-

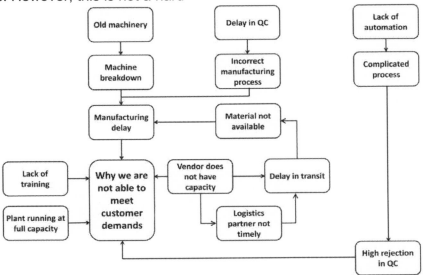

Fig: An interrelationship digraph that analyzes why a company is not able to meet customer demands
and-fast rule.

Sometimes, even key issues may have only a few arrows. Therefore, no issue should be ignored. Issues that have more outgoing arrows are regarded as major causes, whereas issues that have more incoming arrows are regarded as major effects.

Share the uses of Interrelationship Digraphs?

Interrelationship digraphs are used by organizations in different situations for varying purposes.

They are generally used for:
- Analysing any kind of relationship, besides cause-and-effect relationships.
- Analysing complex issues involving several interrelated issues.
- Determining areas of improvement that will have the greatest impact on the organization.
- Analysing logical relationships.
- Analysing problems where causes cannot be organized as hierarchies or matrices.
- Analysing a problem that is believed to be caused by another problem.
- And, developing a better understanding of the relations identified using tools such as affinity diagrams.

How to Create an Interrelationship Digraph?

To create an interrelationship digraph for identifying relationships among different factors:
1. Write the statement defining the problem or issue to be explored through the interrelationship digraph on a card or sticky note.
2. Generate all possible factors of relationships pertaining to the basic problem using:
    a. Brainstorming or;
    b. Affinity diagrams or;
    c. Fishbone diagrams.
3. Write all the identified factors on cards or sticky notes.
4. Place these cards or sticky notes on the work surface one by one after the team discusses the relationship between a card to be placed and all the other cards already placed.
5. After arranging all the cards, draw a relationship arrow from a cause item to an effect item.
6. Repeat this activity for all the cards.
7. If necessary, make several revisions to discuss and discover the cause-and-effect relationships that exist between all the factors.
8. Shortlist the factors to which most arrows point as possible factors for improvement.
9. Discuss and determine the factor that causes most of the problems.

. . . . .

Tree Diagram

In the previous topic, you created an interrelationship digraph. A tree diagram is used to break down crucial components or elements into finer details during a Six Sigma project. In this topic, you will create a tree diagram to analyze processes for identifying the cause of a problem. After identifying key issues, you need to break generalities down to specific details.

A tree diagram that shows the hierarchical structure of tasks that need to be performed to accomplish a particular objective helps you perform a detailed analysis of a process.

What is a Tree Diagram?

A *tree diagram* is a management and planning tool used for breaking down an issue into finer levels of detail. This involves a series of steps where each step progressively breaks an item into its constituent parts. The main or general issue is placed at one end, and specific factors that cause, contribute, or relate to the general issue are placed in the next column and connected by lines. The specifics of each of these smaller issues are placed in the column at the next level. This process is repeated until the issue is broken down to the smallest level possible.

In addition, the tree diagram is used to identify the subcomponents of a process. As the output resembles a tree with one element branching into two or more smaller units, it is called a tree diagram. A tree diagram can be constructed vertically or horizontally.

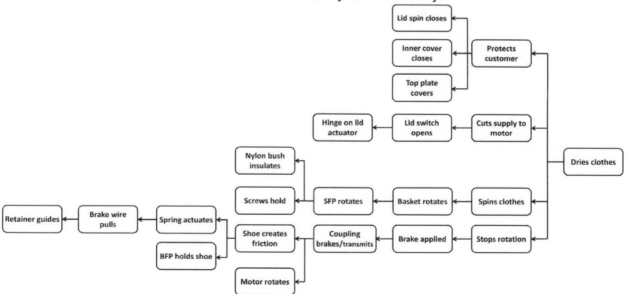

Fig: A tree diagram that illustrates how each part contributes to the primary function of clothes drier

What are the uses of Tree Diagrams?

Tree diagrams are used by organizations when probing an issue or process further. They are generally used for:

- Analysing business processes comprehensively.
- Identifying minute details when progressing from generalities to specifics.
- Finding the root cause of a problem.
- Breaking down a problem that is hierarchical in nature.
- Planning for simplifying a task into smaller and manageable elements.
- Determining steps for implementing a solution.
- And, further analysing the crucial issues identified using an affinity diagram or Interrelationship Digraph.

How to create a Tree Diagram?

To create a tree diagram for breaking down general categories of tasks into finer details:

1. Develop and write down the statement of the goal, project, or problem being analysed.
2. Gather the team that will be involved in creating the tree diagram.
3. Ask an appropriate question that will lead the team to the next level of detail. Questions could focus on:
   a. The tasks that need to be performed to accomplish a goal.
   b. The means of completing a project.
   c. The causes of a problem.
   d. The components of a project.
4. Identify a possible answer to each question by:
   a. Brainstorming among team members or;
   b. Using affinity diagrams.
5. Consider the answers identified at the previous level as the statement for the next level.
6. Follow Steps 3 and 4 to arrive at the next level of detail.
7. Repeat the same process until all basic elements of the goal, project, or problem are identified.

■ ■ ■ ■ ■

Prioritization Matrix

In the previous topic, you created a tree diagram. Key issues identified must also be sorted in the order of their importance. A prioritization matrix helps determine the order for dealing with different issues or selecting solutions according to their relative importance. In this topic, you will create a prioritization matrix to identify crucial issues that require immediate attention.

You must prioritize key issues identified according to their importance to determine which issues or solutions are the most critical and need to be addressed first. Using a prioritization matrix, you can determine such crucial areas where Six Sigma projects need be implemented to improve your business processes.

What are Prioritization Matrices?

A *prioritization matrix* is a tool used for determining the most important issues or solutions. This tool can be used for any prioritization activity. In a Six Sigma project, it can be used for filtering or prioritizing either causes or solutions. For example, the cause-and-effect matrix is a prioritization matrix used for prioritizing causes, while the criteria-based matrix is used for prioritizing solutions.

Whatever the matrix, the procedure used for prioritization is the same. The Six Sigma team identifies different criteria to be used for measuring different solutions. The relative importance of each criterion is determined and a numerical value indicating the weight of each criterion is entered in a column. Ratings are then assigned to the solutions against different criteria. The different solutions are scored against the identified criteria. Each rating is then multiplied by the criteria weights to obtain the weighted scores. The weighted scores are then added to find the cumulative value. The option with the highest total value is regarded as the option with the highest priority.

		Ratings			Weighted Scores		
	Weightage	Solution 1	Solution 2	Solution 3	Solution 1	Solution 2	Solution 3
High Accuracy and Precision	10	8	7	9	80	70	90
Promise to Delivery	9	6	7	8	54	63	72
Reliability	7	9	8	9	63	56	63
Cost	8	8	9	5	64	72	40
Program Management	7	5	4	6	35	28	42
Turnaround Time	5	4	4	6	20	20	30
				Total	316	309	337

Fig: A sample prioritization matrix

What are the uses of Prioritization Matrices?

- Prioritizing complex issues involving several criteria against which the issues are assessed.
- Assigning scores to the criteria or issues when data is available.
- Choosing key areas to be focused upon immediately.
- And, garnering team support and approval of crucial issues.

How to Create a Prioritization Matrix?

To create a prioritization matrix for determining key areas where Six Sigma projects need be implemented first:

1. Gather the team members required to participate in the exercise.
   a. It is not necessary to limit the team to only the project team members.
   b. Involve all stakeholders who would have influence on the items to be prioritized.
   c. Ideally, the size of the team should be around eight.
   d. Agree upon the scope and the duration of the exercise because there is a tendency to drift from the main subject of interest, which may consume more time.
2. Identify criteria against which the items to be prioritized can be weighed. Select the criteria according to your business and the nature of the process.
3. Assign weights to the criteria on a scale of 1 to 10.
   a. Use an ascending scale while assigning the weight. Usually, the higher the better.
   b. Draw consensus within the team on the weights.
4. Assign ratings for each item to be prioritized against different criteria on a scale of 1 to 10. Alternatively, the team can also pick solutions one by one and gather votes for each criterion. Members who agree that a solution fits a particular criterion vote for it. Ensure that necessary information is available to the team before voting.
5. Compute the total score for each item.
   a. Multiply the rating for an item by the weight.
   b. Add the total scores for each item.
6. Continue doing this for every criterion of all the items.
7. Shortlist the items with higher scores for implementation.

• • • • •

Matrix Diagram

In the previous topic, you created a prioritization matrix. A matrix diagram is another important tool used in a project to identify how different categories of data are related to each other. In this topic, you will describe a matrix diagram.

One of the reasons for organizing data is that it helps you analyze data. The matrix diagram that depicts the relationship between different categories of data helps you better interpret the data.

What are Matrix Diagrams?

A *matrix diagram,* also called a *matrix chart,* is a management and planning tool used for identifying relationships between two to four groups of elements or among elements in a single group. The elements in different groups are placed in rows and columns and relationships among them are analysed by the team. Symbols indicating the strength of the relationships are then entered in the cell where the row and column of the two elements intersect. If there is no relationship, then it is left blank. Because matrix diagrams help you analyze data, they are also extensively used in the Measure and Analyze phases of the DMAIC methodology.

What are the different types of Matrix Diagrams?

Matrix diagrams can be sorted into several types depending on the number of data sets being compared.

- **L-shaped** Relates two sets of elements to one another or a single set of elements to itself.
- **T-shaped** Relates three sets of elements where there is no relation between the two sets that are related to a common set.
- **Y-shaped** Relates three sets of elements where one set is related to the other two sets in a circular manner.
- **C-shaped** relates three sets of elements simultaneously.
- **X-shaped** relates four sets of elements.
- **Roof-shaped** relates one set of elements to itself.

What is L-Shaped Matrix Diagram?

The *L-shaped matrix* is a matrix diagram that directly relates two sets of elements (say A and B) to each other or a single set of elements to itself (say A and A). Because the diagram resembles an inverted "L" with a main row and a main column, it is called an L-shaped matrix. It is the most basic kind of matrix diagram and commonly used.

	Americas	**EMEA**	**Asia**	**Pacific**
Misfeed rate	<40 PPM	<40 PPM	<100 PPM	<100 PPM
Multi-feed rate	<50 PPM	<50 PPM	<50 PPM	<50 PPM
Jam rate	<100 PPM	<100 PPM	<500 PPM	<100 PPM
Copy rate	100 copies per min	100 copies per min	60 copies per min	100 copies per min
Jam clearance rate	<20 sec	<30 sec	<1 min	<20 sec
Paper damage rate	<20 PPM	<20 PPM	<20 PPM	<20 PPM
Unit cost	<$5,000	<$6,000	<$3,000	<$4,000

Fig: An L-shaped matrix that summarizes the requirement for a photocopier from customers

What is T-Shaped Matrix Diagram?

The *T-shaped matrix* is a matrix diagram that relates three sets of elements where there is no relation between the two sets that are related to a common set. Here, the sets B and C are related to a common third set, A. However, B and C are not related to one another. This matrix is called a T-shaped matrix because the main column or row is separated along the center by a single row or column, resembling the letter "T." The elements of the common set A are entered on the main row of the matrix. The elements in set B are on the top half of the main column above the main row and the elements in set C are on the bottom half of the main column. By analysing the matrix in different ways, you can gather different information. The T-shaped matrix is also widely used like the L-shaped matrix.

2011	L	H	M	L
2012	L	H	M	M
2013	M	H	M	H
2014	H	H	H	H
Estimated Market Potential **High (H)** **Medium (M)** **Low (L)**	**Model 1**	**Model 2**	**Model 3**	**Model 4**
Americas	L	M	H	M
EMEA	L	M	H	H
Asia	H	H	M	L
Pacific	L	L	M	L

Fig: A T-shaped matrix that summarizes the requirements for different models of photocopiers

What is Y-Shaped Matrix Diagram?

The *Y-shaped matrix* is a matrix diagram that relates three sets of elements where one set is related to the other two sets in a circular manner. . It can be formed by bending the columns of sets A and B in the T-matrix in such a way that there is an interrelation between the elements of these two sets.

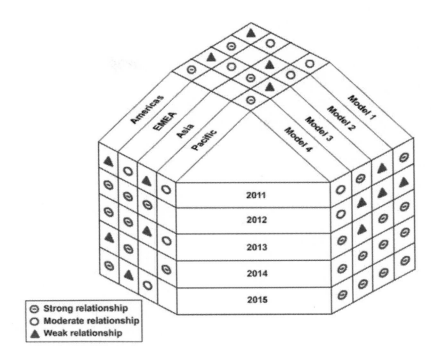

Fig: A Y-shaped matrix that summarizes the requirements for different models of photocopiers

What is C-Shaped Matrix Diagram?

The *C-shaped matrix* is a three-dimensional matrix diagram that relates three sets of elements simultaneously. The "C" in its name stands for "cube." Because drawing a C-shaped matrix is difficult, organizations rarely use this matrix and opt for three-dimensional models of computer software that

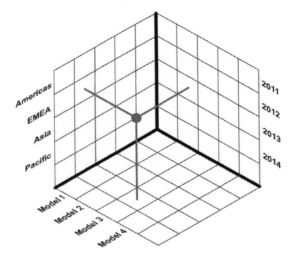

Fig: A C-shaped matrix that summarizes the requirements for different models of photocopiers delivers a clear visual depiction if they want to compare three sets at the same time.

What is X-Shaped Matrix Diagram?

The *X-shaped matrix* is a matrix diagram that relates four sets of elements. Each set is related to two other sets in a circular manner. However, each axis of the matrix is related only to the two adjacent axes and not to those across them. (but not or). The X-shaped matrix is nothing but two T-shaped matrices placed back-to-back and can be formed by extending the T-shaped matrix. Just like the C-shaped matrix, the X-shaped matrix is also rarely used in organizations.

L	H	M	**2011**	L	H	M	L
L	H	M	**2012**	L	H	M	M
M	H	M	**2013**	M	H	M	H
H	H	H	**2014**	H	H	H	H
Manufacturing Plants				**Estimated Market Potential**			
Plant 1	**Plant 2**	**Plant 3**	**High (H) Medium (M) Low (L)**	**Model 1**	**Model 2**	**Model 3**	**Model 4**
L	M	H	**Americas**	L	M	H	M
L	M	H	**EMEA**	L	M	H	H
H	H	M	**Asia**	H	H	M	L
L	L	M	**Pacific**	L	L	M	L

Fig: An X-shaped matrix that summarizes the requirements for a photocopier model

What is a Roof-Shaped Matrix Diagram?

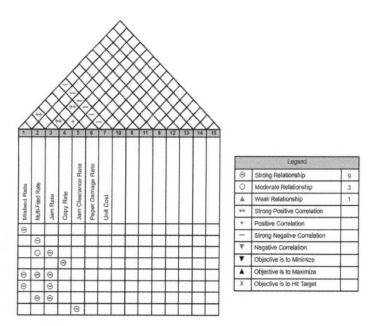

Fig: A roof-shaped matrix that summarizes the relationship of technical specifications

The *roof-shaped matrix* is a matrix diagram that relates one set of elements to it. It is generally used with an L- or a T-shaped matrix. In the roof-shaped matrix, and also in an L- or a T-shaped matrix. It is also used with a House of Quality (HOQ), with the matrix forming the roof of the house.

Describe the uses of Matrix Diagrams.

Matrix diagrams are generally used for identifying:
- Relationships among different sets of items by comparing them, especially many-to-many relationships among them instead of one-to-one relationships.
- The strength of the relationship between different sets of items qualitatively.
- And, the success of a process that generates one set of items from another set of items.

· · · · ·

Process Decision Program Chart (PDPC)

In the previous topic, you created a matrix diagram. After categorizing and prioritizing different issues related to a Six Sigma project, the potential risks associated with the project also need to be identified. A Process Decision Program Chart (PDPC) is an important tool used during the Define phase for identifying risks that may affect the project later. In this topic, you will draft a PDPC.

Before implementing a Six Sigma project, you must identify potential risks that may arise later in the project. Using a PDPC, you can identify risks associated with bottom-level tasks and devise contingency plans and countermeasures to prevent these problems.

Explain PDPC

The *Process Decision Program Chart (PDPC)* is a management and planning tool used to identify potential problems that may arise in a project as well as solutions or countermeasures to address those problems. It is a structured tree diagram with multiple levels for different purposes. It is usually developed from a tree diagram that has up to three levels of activities involved in accomplishing a task. The first, and highest, level shows the objective, and the second level shows the main activities. In the third level, the activities at the second level are divided further to show broadly defined tasks to be performed for accomplishing the main activities.

In many cases, the second and third levels may also coexist as a single level.

The Six Sigma project team brainstorms to anticipate problems that may happen for each task at the third level. These problems are entered as the fourth level. Solutions or countermeasures for each potential problem are then identified through brainstorming and are entered as the fifth level.

What are the uses of a PDPC?

- Before implementing a large and complex plan.
- For identifying potential risks to complete a project successfully.
- For identifying and choosing preventive steps to eliminate potential risks.
- And, when the project is crucial and the consequences of failure are disastrous.

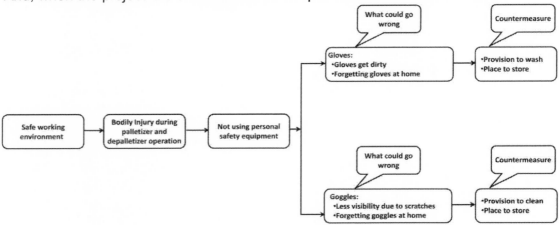

Fig: A partially filled PDPC created while planning safety of employees at workplace

How to Draft a PDPC?

To draft a PDPC for identifying risks that may arise in a project later and countermeasures to eliminate them:

1. Study the high-level tree diagram developed earlier to determine the objective or project to be accomplished.
    1. Note that the main objective is in the first level of the tree diagram.
    2. Note that the main activities that need to be performed to meet the objective are in the second level.
    3. Note that the tasks that need to be performed to accomplish the main activities are in the third level. The levels in a PDPC may differ according to the levels in the tree diagram.
2. Brainstorm the potential problems that could arise for the tasks in the third level and enter them in the fourth level.
3. Review all the potential problems and eliminate solutions that are improbable would have insignificant consequences before entering them in the fourth level.
4. Brainstorm countermeasures for these potential problems, analyze the solutions against criteria such as effectiveness, cost, and time to distinguish practical   countermeasures from impractical ones, and enter them in the fifth level.

▪ ▪ ▪ ▪ ▪

84

Activity Network Diagram

In the previous topic, you drafted a PDPC. After identifying the potential risks associated with the project, you must create a schedule for the project. An activity network diagram is used during the Define phase to plan a schedule. In this topic, you will create an activity network diagram.

Before implementing a Six Sigma project, you need to plan a schedule, taking into account all the tasks and subtasks in it. Using an activity network diagram, you can determine the timelines of the subtasks associated with your project.

An *activity* is an element of project work that requires action to produce a *deliverable.* Activities lay the foundation for estimating, scheduling, executing, and monitoring and controlling the project work. The characteristics of an activity are:

- It has an expected duration and can be scheduled.
- It consumes budgetary and human resources, and so its cost can be determined.
- And, it can be assigned to an individual person or a group.

Example:

In a project that involves building a factory, some examples of activities are:

- Complete soil studies.
- Obtain approval for the design.
- Order a production boiler through an overseas supplier.
- And, install a pollution control system.

Each of these items requires action to produce a deliverable. Each has an expected duration and will consume budgetary and human resources.

A *milestone* is a control point event in a project with zero duration that triggers a reporting requirement or requires sponsor or customer approval before proceeding with the project. Milestones serve as markers and are defined by the project manager, customer, or both. Milestones are also referred to as events.

Define Activity Network Diagrams.

An *activity network diagram* is a graphical representation of the sequence of project activities and dependencies among them. Activity network diagrams read from left to right or top to bottom and are typically accompanied by summary information. The diagram can include either the entire project or just specific parts of it. Parts of an activity network diagram may be referred to as a sub network or a fragmented network.

Summary information describes the basic approach to sequencing project activities.

Activity network diagrams may differ in that they may be:

- Detailed or high level.
- Generated manually or with software.
- Constructed using a variety of methods.

- And, of several types, including the arrow diagramming and precedence diagramming methods.

What are the uses of Activity Network Diagrams?

Activity network diagrams are used primarily while planning and preparing the schedule for the project. They are generally used when the different steps in a project, their sequence, and the duration of each step is clear. Preparing the project schedule is a crucial task because completing a project early or late affects an organization significantly. While organizations stand to gain by completing a project early, failure to complete a project on time will have an adverse impact. Activity network diagrams can be used to:

- Plan a project or activity that has a set of interdependent tasks.
- Understand and describe the activities in a work process clearly.
- Schedule and monitor tasks in a complex project.
- Calculate the earliest date of completing a project and identify the means to alter it, if need be.
- Identify risks to completing a project on time and eliminate them.
- And, communicate the project plan and the risks involved to the team.

How to Create an Activity Network Diagram

To create an activity network diagram:

- Determine the dependencies among project activities.
- Determine the leads and lags between activities.
- Identify predecessor and successor activities.
- Create nodes for all activities with no predecessor activities or dependencies.
- Create nodes for all activities that are successor activities to the nodes already created.
- Draw arrows from predecessor activities to successor activities.
- Continue drawing the network diagram, working from left to right until all activities are included on the diagram and their precedence relationships are indicated by arrows.
- Verify the accuracy of your diagram.

. . . . .

6 Key Metrics in Six Sigma Projects

In this lesson, you will identify key metrics of Six Sigma. Whenever you implement new steps or changes in a process, you need to closely monitor how the changes affect performance. You begin by tracking the performance of a process using different parameters. In this topic, you will track process performance. Any process implementation aligns to a set of redefined organizational goals and characteristics that impact customers and businesses.

Track Process Performance

Your role as a Six Sigma Green Belt is to identify opportunities for improvement in a process. Tracking process performance using different parameters will help you determine the quality of a product or service.

DPU (Defects Per Unit)

Defects Per Unit (DPU) is the average number of defects detected on a specified number of units of a product or service. The formula for calculating DPU is:

Total number of defects / Total number of product units.

Defects

A defect is defined as unacceptable variation from specified standards or customer requirements. It can also be due to the variation of a quality attribute from company-specified standards. Defects in a product or service lead to customer discontent. They may also render the product or service unfit for use.

Defective Units

A defective unit of a product or process contains one or more defects.

Opportunities

Opportunities are defined as a measure of all possible occurrences of defects in a process. They must be independent of each other and measurable. Opportunities are essentially the number of aspects of a product or service that are required to meet customer expectations in which defects can occur. The complexity of a product or service can be determined by the total number of opportunities existing in that product or service.

DPMO

Defects Per Million Opportunities (DPMO), a measure of process performance, is the average number of defects across a million opportunities that a current process will produce. The formula for calculating DPMO is

(No. of defects x1,000,000)/(No. of units x No. of opportunities per unit)

where the number of defects is the total number of defects found in a process, the number of units is the total number of units produced, and the number of opportunities per unit is the number of ways to generate defects.

Sigma Levels

A *Sigma level* is a metric that helps determine the quality level of a process output. The six different Sigma levels are One Sigma, Two Sigma, Three Sigma, Four Sigma, Five Sigma, and Six Sigma. A Sigma level is also called Sigma Capability and is expressed as a number, usually restricted to the first decimal. The higher the Sigma level, the lower the defect level of the process output. Sigma levels are determined based on the defect rate in a process.

DPMO and Sigma Levels

You can convert DPMO to Sigma values using the Yield to Sigma Conversion table. The following table includes details about DPMO pertaining to different Sigma levels.

DPMO	Sigma Level
691,462	1.0
308,538	2.0
66,807	3.0
6,210	4.0
233	5.0
3.4	6.0

As the Sigma level increases, the DPMO of the process drastically decreases. Organizations operating at higher Sigma levels produce substantially fewer defects and will have very high customer satisfaction levels.

Impact of Sigma Levels

Sigma levels determine the maturity level of a process. Process improvements are easy with a new process because there are more opportunities to find flaws, and flaws are often obvious. But, at later stages, it is increasingly challenging to identify opportunities for improvement because a mature process has already undergone many fixes.

Therefore, Sigma levels below Four Sigma involve gathering general data that is less discrete in nature. On the other hand, Four Sigma and Five Sigma levels involve process characterization and optimization and deal with continuous data.

For Sigma levels Five Sigma and Six Sigma, improvement opportunities are very difficult to identify. Therefore, the Design for Six Sigma (DFSS) methodology is used to deal with continuous data related to the process.

RTY

Rolled Throughput Yield (RTY) is the probability that any unit can go through a number of processes without revealing any defects during quality inspection. RTY is the overall process quality that summarizes DPMO data for the entire process. It is an important metric used for processes that require excessive rework, and it serves as a baseline score in the Measure phase and a final score in the Control phase of Six Sigma projects.

COPQ

Cost of Poor Quality (COPQ) is the cost involved in producing defective products or services. This is different from conventional thinking, which assumes that a defective product corrected or caught before it is dispatched to customers is good enough. However, COPQ goes several levels above this thinking and includes:

- The cost involved in bridging the gap between the desired quality and the actual quality of a product or service.
- The cost of lost opportunity because of expending resources to rectify defects.
- And, the labor cost, rework cost, disposition cost, and material cost that have been added to a unit until its rejection.

Elements of COPQ

The elements of COPQ include prevention cost, appraisal cost, and failure cost.

COPQ Element	Description
Prevention cost	• The cost of activities associated with the prevention of poor quality in products or services.
Appraisal cost	• The cost associated with measuring, evaluating, or auditing products and services to ensure conformance to organizational and customer quality standards and to regulatory requirements.
Failure cost	• The cost associated with nonconformance or defective products or services as per customer requirements. • Classified as internal failure cost and external failure cost. • Internal failure cost is associated with the cost that occurs prior to the delivery of goods or services to customers. • External failure cost is associated with the cost that occurs after a product or service reaches customers.

• • • • •

Perform FMEA

In the previous topic, you identified the key metrics that are used to track the performance of a process. During the course of tracking process performance, you will come across risks that impact performance. In this topic, you will perform Failure Modes and Effects Analysis (FMEA) in order to assess such risks.

New initiatives and innovations attract known and unknown risks. When implementing Six Sigma, you require expertise in providing effective solutions whenever risks occur. Your command of assessing risks by using techniques such as FMEA helps you identify various causes leading to the failure of a process and take appropriate actions to mitigate risks.

What is FMEA?

Failure Modes and Effects Analysis (FMEA) is a type of analysis that helps you identify various causes that lead to the failure of a system. Though FMEA is typically used in engineering contexts, it can also be used to identify risks by analysing the causes behind the impact of risks. When determining the probability of failure of the overall system, FMEA indicates the level of quality for a system or product.

In addition, FMEA can be applied to products, designs, or processes. Because FMEA provides an overview of process risks, it can be used as a template that can be updated regularly so that the project team or management is aware of current risks and their priority.

What is DFMEA?

Design Failure Modes and Effects Analysis (DFMEA) is an analytical technique that applies the FMEA method to ensure that potential failure modes and their causes in a design have been identified and addressed. It is conducted by a cross-functional team during the initial stages of designing or while considering major design changes.

The main purpose of performing DFMEA is to ensure that the design can be developed in a cost effective way and is capable of performing along expected lines in a given environment. Moreover, it also ensures that potential failures are identified and corrective measures are applied to eliminate failure. Corrective measures could include changing the design or material and updating performance specifications.

DFMEA focuses on developing and guiding a logical design process and determining and quantifying design risks to reduce the probability of failure. It offers a platform for continuous product improvement and justifies design activities in an organization. It also offers a document for design and development.

Describe the benefits of DFMEA.

The benefits of DFMEA include:

- Identifying potential failures and corrective measures through an unbiased analysis.
- Evaluating the impact of the identified failure modes and their effects on the design or system.
- Prioritizing corrective measures for reducing potential failures.
- And, improving the reliability of the design by reducing the probability of potential failures.

What is PFMEA?

Process Failure Modes and Effects Analysis (PFMEA) is an analytical technique that applies the FMEA method to ensure that potential failures and their causes in a process have been considered and addressed before launching production. It focuses on evaluating each process step and identifying ways in which the process can fail. The potential failures are then evaluated and ranked.

PFMEA also determines the impact of these failures on the end result and identifies the means of eliminating these failures. Though PFMEA is mostly used in manufacturing processes, it can be used to evaluate any existing or new process. PFMEA should be conducted at the earliest possible time in the manufacturing development cycle to gain optimal results. It should also be applied to each manufacturing operation, from individual components to assemblies.

Describe the benefits of PFMEA?

PFMEA offers a number of benefits to organizations by eliminating errors and preventing problems. The benefits of PFMEA include:
- Process enhancement.
- Elimination of waste and non-value-added activities.
- Reduction in cycle time, because time and effort is not wasted on rectifying errors but spent on preventing problems.
- Savings in cost due to elimination of rework, retests, and costs spent on producing defective products or services.
- Improved monitoring of process performance and equipment.
- Improved customer satisfaction due to better product quality and safety.
- And, effective planning for preventing process failure.

Differentiate between DFMEA and PFMEA?

Both DFMEA and PFMEA have similar principles and follow identical steps. Both involve identifying potential failures, their impact, and corrective measures to be taken for reducing or eliminating these potential failures.

However, DFMEA and PFMEA differ in a few aspects, such as their focus and the stage in which these two analyses are done.

DFMEA focuses on potential failures related to product design changes. The main focus is on finding potential failures that can result in malfunctions and safety hazards while using the product. It is also applied to identify potential causes that may curtail the life of the product. It **must** be conducted throughout the entire design process, starting at the preliminary design as soon as the design concept has been selected to the production.

PFMEA focus on potential failures associated with processes and changes to them. The main focus is on finding potential failures related to a process that can affect the quality of a product or cause safety or environmental hazards and result in customer dissatisfaction. It is also applied to identify potential causes that reduce the reliability of the process.

Item	Description
Focus	• DFMEA: On potential failures related to product design changes • PFMEA: On potential failures associated with processes and changes to them
Stage	• DFMEA: Throughout the entire design process • PFMEA: Before launching a new process

What are the elements of Risk?

All forms of risks, be they risks related to a project or risks related to natural hazards, include several elements. They are:
- Context, which describes the background, situation, or environment pertaining to a risk.
- Actions, which are the acts or occurrences that trigger the risk.
- Conditions, which define the current state or circumstances that can lead to the risk.
- And, consequences, which are the potential results or effects of an action.

Define Failure Modes

A failure mode is a mechanism by which a process or system breaks down. Thus, a failure mode can be considered a cause of a problem because it directly affects customers. Every process has its own constraints that are triggers for a possible failure.

Define Effects of Failure Modes

Failure modes can have an effect on processes and customer-related services. Because these impact customers directly, it is obvious that the effects of failure modes impact an organization's business results. Therefore, it is vital to anticipate these effects and to take appropriate remedial actions. In general, effects are rated in terms of their severity. Effects with high severity pose greater risk to customers, processes, or businesses than effects with low severity.

Define Potential Causes of Effects Due to Failure Modes

There are several potential causes of effects that lead to failure modes. Some of these causes related to manufacturing are methods, manpower, materials, money, environment, and machines; and some of the causes related to administration are policies, procedures, and places. You can use specific tools to identify the causes of effects, and you can narrow down the most likely causes through data collection and rule out the non-contributing causes. In general, causes are rated by their frequency of occurrence. Causes that occur frequently pose greater risk than those that occur less frequently.

Define Current Controls on Causes

Controls detect causes or prevent their occurrence. Controls can help determine appropriate corrective actions. In general, control mechanisms built into processes are rated by their detectability. Processes with high failure detectability pose less risk than processes with low detectability.

Elaborate the role of FMEA in Risk Assessment

Failure Modes and Effects Analysis (FMEA) is a risk assessment tool used to analyze potential reliability problems in a process. This tool performs a bottom-up approach toward achieving its objectives. In any process, FMEA identifies potential failure modes such as errors or defects in the process that affect customers, determines their immediate effects or consequences on the product, and identifies the necessary actions to be taken to mitigate the failures.

FMEA prioritizes failure modes based on the frequency of occurrence, the seriousness of consequences, and the ease of detection. It also documents various risks of failures that are associated with continuous process improvement. Due to its importance and the dynamic nature of processes, FMEA is a live document that becomes the risk register for the process.

Define RPN

The *Risk Priority Number (RPN)* is a measure used when prioritizing potential risks associated with a project. The probability of occurrence (P); impact (I), which is also known as severity; and detectability (D); are the parameters taken into account when determining the RPN. Using these parameters, you can calculate the RPN for a risk event by using the formula:
$RPN = P \times I \times D$.
A potential cause with the highest RPN indicates that it will greatly impact the project. Thus, you can plan corrective actions for such causes.

How to Perform FMEA?

To draft an FMEA template:
1. Refer to the process map and analyze each step in the process along with its inputs and outputs.

2. Identify ways in which the process step can fail. If required, refer to the fishbone diagram that represents all the causes of problems.
3. Describe the anticipated failure mode.
4. Describe the effects of the failure.
5. Describe the causes of the effects.
6. Estimate the frequency of occurrence, severity, and detection of failure.
7. Calculate the RPN for each potential failure mode based on values assigned for occurrence, severity, and detectability.
8. As a rule of thumb, determine failure modes with RPN ratings greater than 100.
9. Recommend appropriate actions to reduce the risk of failure.
10. Identify team members for the implementation of recommended actions and determine the appropriate duration.
11. Update the FMEA template based on the changes to the process and changes in P, I, D, and RPN.

■ ■ ■ ■ ■

7 Six Sigma Team Stages and Dynamics

During the stages of team development, a team goes through various patterns of evolving and bonding. Identifying these patterns will help you develop a high-performing Six Sigma project team and drive your Six Sigma project successfully. In this topic, you will define and describe the various Six Sigma project team stages and team dynamics.

A team becomes effective only when all the members bond and work as one toward a specific goal. As a Six Sigma Green Belt, one of your primary tasks is to develop an effective project team and channel it toward achieving Six Sigma goals. This will help you develop an effective Six Sigma project team and complete the project successfully.

Team Development

Irrespective of processes or skills, a team takes time to evolve into a cohesive unit. Team development follows clearly defined paths and undergoes various stages. At each stage, teams exhibit unique characteristics and a recognizable pattern of behavior. These characteristics and behavior patterns form a framework to identify and understand changes in a team's behavior and help maximize its process and productivity. There are many models that frame team behavior. Traditionally, most of them suggested that team development occurs in four stages. Now, it is universally accepted that there are six stages in team development.

Describe the stages of Team Evolution

A team goes through a process of developing maturity, establishing relationships, and becoming more participative and united with a sense of purpose to see a project to completion, after which they disengage and move on to other projects.

- *Forming* Team members are in an exploratory mood. They cautiously interact with each other and weigh each others' capabilities. At the same time, they learn about their role and the roles of the other members of the team.
- *Storming* Teams experience conflict as members jockey for power and control. This competitive behavior causes a strain in relationships among team members. Team members are keen on exploring their autonomy and arguments over the project and operating procedures flare up.
- *Norming* Team members resolve their differences and become more cohesive. They work as a unit to solve problems and focus on establishing their worth as a team. The team realizes the value of observing basic rules and operating procedures. The team is focused on accomplishing tasks.
- *Performing* Teams become high-performing, problem-solving units. They are highly proactive, requiring very little intervention from management. Teams will demonstrate loyalty and an eagerness to accept disagreements within them.

- *Adjourning* The team has completed the project and is in a laudatory mood. At the same time, they are in the process of being disbanded and reassigned to other projects and teams. Some team members may feel threatened about the change to a new environment.
- *Recognition* Team performance is evaluated against the standards, goals, and objectives of the project. Individuals and teams are recognized for their performance, and feedback is also given. This helps project leaders to understand teams and team processes better.

What is negative dynamics in a team?

Negative dynamics are team dynamics that negatively influence the performance of a team and the quality of a product. Negative dynamics impact a Six Sigma project team's performance by reducing task understanding, creativity, and efficient use of resources.

Sometimes, negative dynamics promote personal growth at the cost of teamwork. They also result in low professional communication and poor organization skills. Negative dynamics create a code of ethics, or an unspoken set of standards, and exercise subtle control over effort and the amount of output. They impede team members' ability to utilize their unique skills on the task at hand and their ability to develop alternative strategies to accomplish goals.

Example: Negative Dynamics at Work.

Peter Brown is an exceptionally knowledgeable and hardworking engineer in an automobile manufacturing organization. Unfortunately, he is often barely civil to his colleagues. His abrupt manner upset a few members of his team and they even requested to be removed from his project. Because each member of the team brought a critical skill to the project, management urged Peter to modify his behavior. Although Peter appeared to have understood the importance of changing his behavior, he continued to undermine the team's morale with his unpleasant personal comments. Because of the negative effect Peter had on the team, they began to fall behind on important tasks. Even though Peter was good at his work, his obnoxious behavior reduced the capacity of the team to perform and delayed the project. This left the organization with no other alternative than to remove Peter from the team.

Describe the different types of Negative Behavior along with impact and solution

Individuals exhibit different types of negative behavior in different situations, which reflects on the team as negative dynamics.

Floundering Teams: Teams flounder most often at the start and at the end of a project. They flounder because they are unclear about the task, uncomfortable with each other, or overwhelmed. This is solved by reviewing the problem and then deciding on the solution. Allotting time to create checklists and effective communication can prevent teams from floundering.

Bullying: Bullying happens when a person wields a disproportionate amount of influence. It can be countered by bringing in a person of higher authority, by reinforcing the importance of teamwork, and by using tools such as brainstorming.

Blabbermouth: They Blabber repeatedly. Take over meetings and discussions by commandeering the conversation and by denying other people the opportunity to express their opinions. This can be overcome by structuring discussions so that everyone can speak and by politely reminding blabbermouths that it is time to hear others' opinions.

Wallflower(s): Wallflower(s) are a person or persons who won't speak or contribute to team discussions. Structure discussions in a way that everyone has to speak. Divide tasks into individual assignments or reports and ask every individual to state their experience. Unsupported facts Self-assured statements are offered without legitimate supporting evidence and often in a way that makes further questioning on the topic impolite. This behavior problem can be countered by asking open-ended questions on the validity of the statement and by asking for supportive data.

Haste: Often reflected by impatience when deciding to do something, often dismissing contrary ideas. Haste can be overcome by restating long-term goals and by setting and enforcing rules of teamwork, such as those for brainstorming.

Discounting: This **occurs** when a team member's ideas are dismissed or his contribution is marginalized. Counter this by reminding the team that everyone's ideas matter. Talk off-line with the person showing dismissive behavior and structure inclusive times when all ideas are volunteered and considered.

Digressing: Sometimes meetings go off tangent into irrelevant discussions. Stop this by working from a written agenda and also by directing the conversation back to the relevant subject.

Feuding :This happens when two team members disagree and the disagreement becomes the sole platform for their work.

Avoid: Avoid putting them together on a task and contract a working arrangement for the two who are battling. If everything fails, appeal to a higher authority to mediate.

- - - - -

Six Sigma Teams and Roles

In the previous topic, you recognized how teams evolve and described the impact of team dynamics. Choosing the right person for a role and allotting responsibilities determine the success of a Six Sigma project. In this topic, you will describe Six Sigma teams and their roles.

Identifying the right participant and designating suitable roles is critically important to successfully completing a Six Sigma project. Done correctly, it will ensure that you meet your performance improvement targets.

How are Six Sigma Team organized?

Six Sigma teams are groups of individuals that bring authority, knowledge, abilities, and skills to successfully implement Six Sigma in an organization. Six Sigma team members with varying backgrounds and talents are guided by implementation leaders.

What is Six Sigma council?

This leadership team acts as a steering committee for the projects. It defines the goals and objectives of the Six Sigma implementation across an organization. The team also defines the purpose of the Six Sigma program by linking Six Sigma goals to enterprise goals, explaining how the results are going to benefit customers, scheduling work and interim deadlines, developing review processes to approve the project selection strategy, and supporting team members and other established positions.

What is a Six Sigma Project team?

This team focuses on the incremental and radical improvement of an entire process. The main areas of improvement are quality, cost, and cycle time. It is comprised of members from different levels in an organization who work with processes on a routine basis. Because their positions vary, members generally report to different supervisors.

A Six Sigma project team is led by a Black Belt or Green belt. He or she guided by Master Black Belt or Black Belt respectively.

Who is a Project Sponsor?

A sponsor, who is part of the Six Sigma council or leadership team, takes ownership of various processes and systems and helps coordinate process improvement activities. Sometimes, this term is interchangeability used with Champion. However a champion is a middle- or senior-level individual who is process owner. They also ensure that resources are available to the team and cross-functional issues among members are resolved.

What the role of Master Black Belt in Six Sigma?

Master Black Belts are highly experienced professionals who act as in-house coaches of the Six Sigma methodology. A Master Black Belt devotes 100% of his or her time to Six Sigma and guides Black Belts and Green Belts in project execution. The responsibilities of a Master Black Belt are to:
- Schedule work for the team.
- Identify and define desired results of a project.

- Ensure that Six Sigma is applied consistently across various functions and departments.
- Mediate conflicts and disagreements.
- Identify the success of a project.

What the role of Black Belt in Six Sigma?

Black Belts are professionals who have achieved the highest skill level of the Six Sigma methodology and are experienced in various projects and techniques. A Black Belt devotes most of his or her time to focus on Six Sigma project execution. The responsibilities of a Black Belt are to:

- Lead improvement efforts on projects.
- Ensure that a specific process is followed for each project.
- Facilitate four to six projects a year with a minimum of two years of assignment commitment.
- Provide training to Green Belts.

What the key responsibilities of a Green Belt?

Green Belts assume the role of project managers. They are individuals responsible for managing all aspects of the project. A Green Belt:

- Works with stakeholders to define the project.
- Plans, schedules, and budgets project activities with team input.
- Works with the team to carry out project plans.
- Monitors performance and takes corrective action.
- Identifies, monitors, and mitigates risks.
- Keeps the sponsor and stakeholders informed.
- Requests and documents scope changes.
- Provides timely reports on project metrics.
- Acts as a liaison between the project team and other stakeholders.

What the role of Yellow Belt in Six Sigma?

An employee who receives training on the basic application of Six Sigma management tools. Yellow Belts are part of the process improvement team and work closely with Black Belts throughout less-complex projects in addition to performing their daily tasks.

What the role of White Belt in Six Sigma?

A professional who possesses general awareness of Six Sigma without formal training. Six Sigma project team members are part of the process improvement team and can bring their relevant expertise to a particular Six Sigma project.

How to interpret various Six Sigma Belt designations?

Belt designations within Six Sigma are descriptive of internal roles and often are job titles, functional designations, or formal professional categories. Anyone with appropriate skills and knowledge can also function at a given belt level. Unlike other quality management methodologies, Six Sigma recognizes individuals rather than the organization or the processes and awards belt certifications to individuals. In organizations that have elaborate resources and staffing for Six Sigma, job titles and functional designations align with belt designations.

Other organizations which are trying out Six Sigma may choose to have a very lean structure and staffing. Such organizations usually start by training their high-potential, fast-track performers, from departments such as operations, manufacturing, and quality, in Six Sigma. Initially, they may be given additional responsibilities. Over time, they are moved into full-time Six Sigma roles. There is no central governing or authorizing body that grants belt designations, but there are many independent training and certification organizations that provide their own Six Sigma belt accreditations.

However, for consistency and quality considerations, it is important to hold an accreditation recognized by a reputed organization for a given belt level so that an individual can represent himself or herself as a professional holding a specific belt.

■ ■ ■ ■ ■

Identify Team Tools

In the previous topic, you identified the Six Sigma project team and assigned appropriate roles. In order to get optimum performance out of the team, it is important to apply the correct team tools. In this topic, you will describe the available team tools.

During the life cycle of a Six Sigma project, you will encounter phases where your project team's input is of vital importance. However, rarely do all members contribute equally. Therefore, it is important that you identify relevant team tools and employ them to get the maximum input from your team.

Define Brainstorming

Brainstorming is a problem-solving technique used by process experts to collectively form ideas that lead to a mutual solution of a problem. It involves contributing uncensored views and ideas in a non-judgemental atmosphere. Brainstorming can be conducted in a formal session with a facilitator or an informal session where the ideas are gathered in the context of the conversation. Through brainstorming, the Six Sigma team members can:
- Identify the significant causes of problems in a process.
- Identify the necessary steps required to eliminate or prevent problems in the process.
- Identify the input required to produce defect-free units of the process.
- Identify the suppliers of the input.

- And, identify the output that meets customer requirements with regard to Quality.

Example: Brainstorming to Identify Causes of Problems.
OGC, a computer manufacturer, recently implemented the Six Sigma methodology to improve the quality of its products. A Six Sigma team was formed to identify the potential areas to be improved in the process. The company appointed a facilitator to organize and run a brainstorming session. Through brainstorming, the Six Sigma team identified significant causes of problems in the process and the necessary steps required to prevent such problems in the future. This enabled the team to design the product in such a way that it meets customer requirements.

What is NGT (Nominal Group Technique)?
The *Nominal Group Technique (NGT)* is a structured variation of group brainstorming that encourages everyone to state their opinions. This technique helps resolve issues or problems that require a rapid consensus by reducing interactions among team members to the minimum and using voting to arrive at a consensus.

NGT is used to:
- Prevent the more vocal group members from dominating discussions.
- Provide some group members the space to think.
- Enable passive members to participate in decision-making.
- Facilitate the generation of a number of ideas.
- Enable new members of the team to participate.
- And, resolve controversial issues and reduce heated arguments.

Example: NGT to Reduce Cost-Per-Product. During a discussion on reducing cost-per-product, the line manager noticed that a few members were silent. It also came to light that there was no consensus. He decided to run an NGT session to get everyone to state their opinions and identify a solution. Based on the votes, the team decided to target value engineering and negotiate with vendors to reduce the cost of raw materials and cost-per-product.

What is Multi-Voting technique?
Multi-voting is a structured approach that allows groups to narrow down a long list of ideas and prioritize them for further evaluation. It is used as an evaluating technique when a group has to choose from the ideas generated from a brainstorming session. Multi-voting guarantees a consensus because each member of the team gets to cast multiple votes on a list of items and allows group members to focus on ideas with the maximum potential. It is also called an N/3 voting technique.

For instance, there will be several rounds of voting. In each round, only one-third of the ideas are voted on and the rest are dropped. If there are 100 ideas, it would have been narrowed down to 33 ideas in the first round. After the second round, it would have been reduced to 11 ideas and to three ideas after the third round. Multi-voting is used when:

- A long list of possibilities has been generated through brainstorming.
- A long list of options has to be narrowed down.
- And, a decision must be made by judgment.

Example: Productivity Loss in an Auto Manufacturer's Assembly Line. A process improvement team was formed to address productivity loss in an auto manufacturer's assembly line. Despite prolonged discussions, no clear-cut solution emerged. A brainstorming session was held, resulting in the following list of causes for lost productivity:

- Numerous non-value-added activities present.
- A lack of focus on productivity.
- No incentives for improving productivity.
- No productivity improvement projects.
- A lack of automation.
- Incorrect productivity measurements.
- Surplus workers in each shift.
- The assembly line is working on three shifts.
- An inconsistent supply of raw materials.
- And, no counselling for workers.

The team members were asked to vote and select four chief causes for productivity loss. The following causes were then voted as areas for improvement:

- Non-value-added activities.
- No incentives for improving productivity.
- Incorrect productivity measurements.
- And, an inconsistent supply of raw materials.

After identifying these four areas, the product line manager asked team members to vote and select one or two choices each. The votes were consolidated and non-value-added activities and inconsistent supply of raw materials were identified as the top two reasons for productivity loss. This pared-down list was then sent to the production manager for approval.

■ ■ ■ ■ ■

Identify Effective Communication Techniques

In the previous topic, relevant team tools were identified and used effectively to optimize the performance of the Six Sigma project team members. It is equally important to identify the most appropriate communication techniques for different situations and to ensure the success of your Six Sigma projects. In this topic, you will identify effective communication techniques. Communication is a complex process. Often, there are misunderstandings, and messages are diluted or distorted. In order to prevent a negative impact on the success of a Six Sigma project, the right communication techniques must be applied. So, it is imperative to apply effective communication techniques to overcome barriers to the success of your project.

Explain the role of effective communication in Six Sigma Project?

Effective communication among Six Sigma project team members and stakeholders is crucial to the success of a project. Communication keeps Six Sigma project team members informed about the project's progress, clarifies the methods of executing tasks, and provides feedback. It also provides management with information that facilitates decision making. Communication plays a crucial part in controlling the flow of a project. It helps identify constraints and analyze alternative courses of action.

What are the different types of Communication?

Communicating project information among stakeholders is crucial to the project's success. The type of communication flow depends on the message, the sender, and the user.

Top-down: The top-down flow or the downward flow of communication flows from top management and percolates down the organizational ladder. Communication stating company policies and feedback regarding project progress flows down from the executive sponsor to the champion, then to the Black Belt and Green Belts, and finally to the Six Sigma project team members. To prevent distortions or misunderstandings, top-down communication is sent as written communication. Sometimes, management convenes meetings to communicate to the entire project team.

Bottom-up: The bottom-up flow or upward communication occurs when a line operator wants to provide feedback directly to the executive sponsor. The bottom-up flow of communication is critical because management can draw on ideas generated at the grassroots level and draw up more justifiable plans. The bottom-up flow of communication is prone to distortions, and to prevent it, management convenes stand-up meetings, conducts surveys, and even uses informal devices such as suggestion boxes to facilitate feedback.

Horizontal: The horizontal or sideways flow of communication involves the exchange of information, ideas, and feedback among Six Sigma project team members at the same level in an organization or a project. Horizontal communications are effective in flat organizations and provide quick results. In hierarchic organizations, this type of communication may cause problems because it is independent of managerial intervention.

Explain communication strategy

Communication strategy is a management technique to determine the most effective method for articulating, explaining, and promoting an organization's vision and goals. Communication strategy links diverse activities in a process improvement effort and broadcasts a consistent message that appeals to all stakeholders.

An effective communication strategy ensures the distribution of accurate and timely information critical to the success of the project and promotes and gains support for project improvement.

Example: Communication Strategy for Process Improvement Effort. The improvement team found that the mass of data generated by a project was overshadowing the data showing improvements resulting from the process improvement effort. In order to make the improvement more visible, they decided to provide an executive summary along with every report, not only to management, but also in the information shared with other groups. This strategy crystallized achievements, made data comprehensible, and made gradual improvement in the process more visible.

. . . . .

End of Part One

Made in the USA
Middletown, DE
11 July 2023

34893857R00064